SINGULARITY.AND.CO.

WED-SUN
12-7PM BOOKS

SINGULARITY PULP-SCI-FI
SHOP.COM FANTASY

OFF TRACK PLANET'S

BROOKLYN

TRAVEL GUIDE

-------- for the --------

YOUNG, SEXY, and BROKE

BY THE EDITORS OF OTP

FREDDIE PIKOVSKY
ANNA STAROSTINETSKAYA

RUNNING PRESS
PHILADELPHIA · LONDON

© 2015 by Off Track Planet
Published by Running Press,
A Member of the Perseus Books Group

Books published by Running Press are available at special discounts for bulk purchases in the United States by corporations, institutions, and other organizations. For more information, please contact the Special Markets Department at the Perseus Books Group, 2300 Chestnut Street, Suite 200, Philadelphia, PA 19103, or call (800) 810-4145, ext. 5000, or e-mail special.markets@perseusbooks.com.

ISBN 978-0-7624-5710-6
Library of Congress Control Number: 2014943139

E-book ISBN 978-0-7624-5714-4

9   8   7   6   5   4   3   2   1
Digit on the right indicates the number of this printing

Cover photo © Thinkstock, SaschaHass
Cover design by Freddie Pikovsky
Interior design and illustrations by Adil Dara
Edited by Jordana Tusman
Typography: Archer, Bebas Neue, Mensch, Neutraface, Korolev

Running Press Book Publishers
2300 Chestnut Street
Philadelphia, PA 19103-4371

Visit us on the web!
www.runningpress.com

CONTENTS

INTRODUCTION

These days, Brooklyn is doing a lot more than dying. An eclectic city that was built, and continues to be redefined, by immigrants, Brooklyn is a mystery grab bag of food, fashion, culture, art, music, and wild parties. While Manhattan is mostly all about big business, Brooklyn is still mom-and-pop, with artisans at every corner meticulously crafting local beer, cheese, chocolate, pickles, jewelry, and just about everything else you can eat, wear, or drink. It is the perfect place for our ADD-ridden generation to lay down our roots, because stimulation of some kind is never lacking.

Creating a travel guide that would encompass everything Brooklyn has to offer is impossible. This city changes with the drop of a hat, and that's what makes it special. As such, we pulled out all of our favorite spots—some old-school, some brand-new.

We covered as many neighborhoods as we thought would serve you and included enough pizza joints to shoot your cholesterol through the roof. Our guide isn't traditional, because we're not in the business of spoon-feeding you information. Here are a few tips on how to get the most out of this book.

PREDEPARTURE

We created this section to give you the basics of what you'll need to know before you go. This includes general information about the weather, necessary paperwork like visas, available accommodations, transportation, and money-related issues. Here, we also give you a little heads-up about fashion, politics, and culture so you can pretend you're a Brooklynite right off the bat.

NEIGHBORHOODS

Brooklyn is split into a lot of different neighborhoods, and the understanding of where borderlines are drawn fluctuates depending on whom you ask. Some people will swear that South Park Slope is actually Sunset Park and that most of Clinton Hill is Bed-Stuy. We covered as many neighborhoods as we thought were relevant for the purposes of this guide and grouped them in a way that would be easy for you to navigate. As such, you'll find that some sections cover multiple neighborhoods at a time while others, like Williamsburg, get an entire chapter to themselves. We may get shit for referring to all of East Williamsburg as Bushwick, or for mashing Prospect Heights and Crown Heights together, but from the ground up, you'll find it easier to travel through this tangled town.

RECOMMENDATIONS

There are enough restaurants, bars, venues, and attractions in Brooklyn to keep you busy for a very long time. Instead of giving you a rundown of everything, we chose the places we think would be of most interest to you. Additionally, Brooklyn is full of crossovers, which means that some bars will also have great food, and some coffee shops will serve wine. We've included restaurants made famous on the Food Network, less popular (but just as tasty) joints we love, quirky bars, more expensive places to treat yourself, offbeat activities and sights, street art, poppin' music venues, and all the relevant information you need to track them down. Within each neighborhood, you'll find sections on cafés and bakeries, eateries, shopping options, things to see and do, and places to drink and party. We also threw in some nonfunctional hashtags to sum things up for those of you with little patience for full

sentences. We do not list websites for businesses—because Google it.

HIPSTER HATE

If you can give us an all-encompassing definition of a "hipster" (without sounding like a hipster), we'll send you a handcrafted gold medal. Brooklyn has been bashed for being the epicenter of everything hipster, but the truth is that whatever the scapegoat stereotype really means, Brooklyn is full of creative people who wear funky things and sometimes look poorer than they actually are. You'll have a much better time if you go there with an open mind.

THINGS CHANGE

The cool thing about Brooklyn is that it is in a constant state of change. New businesses open and close in the same month. There are one-off parties, pop-up bars and markets, and seasonal events. We did our best to cover what's current. If a listing in this guide no longer exists once you get there, don't fret; something will open down the street to fill the void. Keep in mind that prices for tickets, passes, and festivals, et cetera are subject to change as well, but are current as of the date of publication of this guide.

Use this guide as a starting point. If you do Brooklyn right, things there will find you, suck you in, feed you, booze you, and only loosen their grip if you beg for mercy. Be it dilapidated warehouses in Bushwick, wine bars in Fort Greene, posh rooftops in Williamsburg, or drink-by-the-river joints in Red Hook, just being in Brooklyn sets you up for a good time.

A BRIEF HISTORY

Brooklyn Navy Yard
is established
1801

1646
Village of Breuckelen
authorized by the Dutch
East India Company

1883
Brooklyn Bridge is built

The residents of Brooklyn are a mash-up of 150 nationalities that speak 136 different languages and identify with 93 different ethnic groups. As such, the history of this place is different depending on whom you ask. The truth is, Brooklyn has always flowed and ebbed, with incredible innovation, culture, community togetherness, and economic booms at the high tides, and racial tension, violence, drugs, and economic depression at the low.

The first official city to get recognition as an independent municipality, the Village of Breuckelen was authorized by the Dutch East India Company in 1646. Then mostly a sparse industrial and agricultural burb, the village was split into six different townships. Many battles of the American Civil War were fought on Brooklyn's soil, remnants of which can be seen at the Old Stone House in Park Slope and Grand Army Plaza.

As the city grew, the economies of all the townships were heavily dependent on the ports along the East River, where the Brooklyn Navy Yard was established in 1801. European immigrants came by the boatloads and found factory jobs in the thriving port. Hot summers pushed cultures onto the streets, where their kids would play and grow up together, creating the beginnings of the multiethnic diversity that would come to define Brooklyn.

By the 1880s, ferries jetted across the river to transport goods and people. In 1883, for ease of transport, the Brooklyn Bridge was built after fourteen years in the making. The bridge brought with it a new set of domestic immigrants from Manhattan, mainly the gentrifying types who were willing to trade longer commutes for lower rents. The more

Brooklyn added to New
York City as one of the
five boroughs
1898

Brooklyn Dodgers
officially play their first
game at Ebbets Field
1913

1899
Al Capone Is born

Brooklyn grew, the farther poorer people were pushed away from the ports. Above ground trolleys and subways were built to facilitate work commutes, and communities settled along these transportation routes. Eventually, all of the townships were unified into Kings County, and in 1898, Brooklyn was added to New York City as one of the five boroughs.

Brooklyn's large factories always had low-skilled jobs available, and newly freed slaves from the South, non-English-speaking immigrants, and nearby Puerto Ricans escaping poverty were able to find work in Brooklyn. Italian family gangs ran a lot of shady businesses from their restaurants, and industry was flourishing, both above- and underground. Until the Great Depression in 1929 when everything went to shit.

Factories shut down, jobs were scarce, and everyone had to learn to hustle. Sports became important to raise morale. While popular since the 1880s, the Brooklyn Dodgers officially played their first game at Ebbets Field in Flatbush in 1913, and despite the team always sort of sucking, the crowds consistently piled in to watch their team. Why pay to see a shitty team? Brooklyn has always been comprised of underdogs, which only became more apparent when economic times were tough, and rooting for the Dodgers was an easy common unifier of Brooklyn's diverse population. Lovingly referred to as "dem bums," the Dodgers were a representation of the people of Brooklyn—the hardworking but not always successful, fun-loving, crazy people of Brooklyn. While racial tension was high elsewhere, the composition of the Dodgers soon began to resemble the true demographic of the team's home

The Dodgers finally
manage to win the
World Series
1955

1929
The Great Depression
(aka when everything
goes to shit)

1957
The Dodgers are
traded to LA

city, with Jackie Robinson (the first black pro baseball player in MLB) added to the team in 1947. The team puttered along, with huge crowds dragging behind them, and finally managed to win one World Series in 1955.

During this same time, Coney Island was a thriving playground for the poor, gaining popularity in 1919, shortly after the extension of the subway line. You could get away from reality and onto the beach for only ten cents and spend an entire day in a land of oddities, diversions, thrills, and greasy hot dogs. While things were tight, times in Brooklyn were fucking fun.

When WWII struck in 1939, Brooklyn tapped into its production abilities to supply the American military with ships, air carriers, and troops. These new jobs were filled by women as men went off to war. When the men returned from war in 1945, things just weren't the same. Those with the means moved to more suburban areas like Queens and Staten Island. Then, in 1957, to further break the Brooklyn spirit, the Dodgers left for LA, which incited all kinds of pissed-off yelling and getting the fuck outta there.

People left, production decreased, the

economy flopped, and the poorest were left to tend the land. The Navy Yard closed and the two-day blackout of 1977 incited mass riots and arson, which added salt to the brink-of-poverty wounds. Many parts of Brooklyn saw a rise in drug use, crime, and unemployment.

As a result of immigration legislature that would allow previously blocked people from the Caribbean from entering the United States, the 1980s brought in a new crowd of poor immigrants from the West Indies, and the following years would see a massive influx of immigrants from China, Russia, Mexico, and Latin America. A whole new jumble of cultures began to rub elbows.

Racial tensions were again high, and people looked for ways to express themselves. While it may have originated in the Bronx, hip-hop got its flavor in Brooklyn. Influenced by West Indian drumbeats, with added complexity using spoken words (or rap) over top, hip-hop rolled into every neighborhood with a stoop. Brooklyn had a lot of words to fuel the fire and stories of poverty, crackheads, drive-bys, and gangsta shit were told via rap

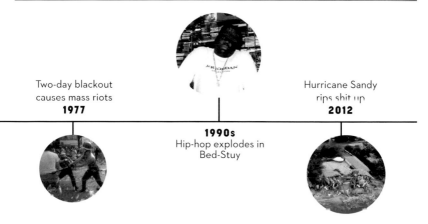

Two-day blackout
causes mass riots
1977

1990s
Hip-hop explodes in
Bed-Stuy

Hurricane Sandy
rips shit up
2012

street battles, most notoriously by Biggie, Talib Kweli, Mos Def, and later Jay Z.

In the mid-'90s, Brooklyn reeled in government funding to deal with the increasing crack problem, and many neighborhoods saw more policing. Gentrification rolled through by 2000 when the Bohemian lifestyle got too expensive to maintain across the bridge and hordes of high kids migrated to enjoy the lower rents of then-exclusively-Hasidic Williamsburg, mostly-Puerto-Rican Bushwick, and still-kind-of-cracked-out Bed-Stuy.

This restarted the cycle of growth and tension. As those with the means to afford higher rents moved into poorer neighborhoods, many others were "priced out" of their longtime homes. Neighborhoods "developed" when new businesses opened to capitalize on the dollars being brought into Brooklyn, themselves enjoying affordable commercial rents.

Gentrification killed a certain part of Brooklyn but allowed for the development of another. The return to small-batch industry, and crafting of artisanal, superspecialized, local goods may be the butt of Brooklyn

jokes, but as a movement it has resurrected something reminiscent of Brooklyn's most productive era. Even with gentrification's dark sides, Brooklyn's sense of community is strong, as evidenced by the events following Hurricane Sandy in 2012, when whole businesses were rebuilt by the kindness of others.

Brooklyn has seen a lot collectively, and Brooklynites will tell you nostalgic stories while bitching about how everything has changed. But that's the beauty of Brooklyn: It changes, and with every transposition, a new flavor is added to each little neighborhood's history. Brooklyn is the story of the underdog, living (and thriving) across the bridge from the richest, most populated city in America.

FUN FACT

If Brooklyn were a stand-alone city, it would be the seventh largest in the country.

PREDEPARTURE

Before you go hard in BK, there are a few things you should know. This city will treat you right if you've got the basics down. We're here to give you some pointers on transportation, health and safety, and accommodations and get you prepped for the madness to come.

VISAS AND DOCS

VISAS

For short visits (ninety days or fewer), the residents of thirty-seven countries fall under the "visa waiver program" and do not need to obtain a visa to enter the United States. After 2006, the passports from these countries come with an integrated chip that will permit entrance without the need of additional documentation. You can check the U.S. Department of State's website to see if your country is on the list.

If you happen to be from, say, Mexico, consider yourself sort of fucked. To get into the United States for any period of time, you'll need to apply for a visa. You first have to fill out Form DS-160, upload a photo, and arrange an interview with your local U.S. embassy (to which you'll need to bring the confirmation page of Form DS-160, a $160 application fee, and an additional issuance fee if applicable).

Longer visits require travelers to apply for certain visas based on their intended purpose in the United States. For all work visas with a known departure time, your prospective employer must submit a petition for your work visa and go through the process with you.

To study in the United States, you must obtain an F-1 or M-1 visa prior to your arrival.

Generally, once you are accepted into a U.S. school, you will be entered into SEVIS (Student and Exchange Visitor Information System) and will need to fill out several forms and pay the I-901 SEVIS fee of $200 (which you can pay online). To obtain your student visa, you will need to fill out all applicable forms, pay fees, and attend an interview. All other student visa information can be found on the U.S. Department of State's website.

DOCUMENTS

No matter what your destination, always travel with copies of your passport, prescriptions, and birth certificate. E-mailing these to yourself is also a good safety precaution.

TRANSPORTATION

FROM THE AIRPORT

Both major airports that service NYC are located in Queens. There is a bastard airport in New Jersey called Newark; if you're coming to Brooklyn from there, you'll take the train to Penn Station and then get on whatever subway you need to hop the river.

John F. Kennedy International Airport

It's five dollars to get out of the airport by public transportation (and another five when you return), and the pass can be purchased in conjunction with a MetroCard at the station kiosks. The AirTrain will take you directly to the subway entrance. The A train services JFK airport, and it's a nice long ride out to Brooklyn (about forty minutes, depending on where you're going). Hopping on the LIRR (Long Island Railroad), a commuter train that services places near and far in New York, is pretty easy. You just ride the AirTrain to Jamaica Station, purchase a ticket at the

LIRR kiosks, and select Atlantic Terminal as your destination. Upon arrival at the Atlantic Terminal, you'll find a handful of subway lines that will take you all around Brooklyn.

LaGuardia Airport

LaGuardia has an old bowling alley feel to it. It's smaller and less busy than JFK and fairly easy to navigate. While there are no subways that directly link up to the airport, there are a few bus options depending on which subway you'd like to connect to. The Q70 limited and Q47 connect to the F, M, R, and 7 trains at Roosevelt Avenue and 74th Street. The M60 connects to the N and Q at Hoyt Avenue and 31st Street. Buses will not take cash. You'll need to buy a Metro-Card to board the bus and then the subway, and there are kiosks around that take cash, credit, and debit.

You can also take a cab (or car service), and it'll cost you $45–$60 one way.

SUBWAY

Like most of NYC, Brooklyn depends heavily on its subway system for daily transportation. There are several options when it comes to purchasing a MetroCard: $112 for a monthly unlimited card; $30 for a weekly unlimited; $2.25 for a single-ride pass; or you can put any denomination of money on the

card (cash, debit, or credit) and use it as you go. A new rule tacks on one dollar for every new, physical MetroCard that you buy (done to eliminate wasted paper cards), so make sure to keep your cards and refill them.

During the day on the weekdays, the trains are extremely reliable and most run every couple of minutes, more frequently during rush hour. At night, the trains still run but much slower. The weekends are a whole different story. Since construction on the NYC subway system is ongoing and reserved for the weekends, the service on many train lines is interrupted (and sometimes entirely suspended) on the weekends. Free shuttle buses are usually set up to replace trains when needed, and you can find all planned construction for the weekends on mta.info. People hate the G train every day of the week. You'll find out why soon enough.

BUSES

Public buses cost $2.25 per trip and accept the same MetroCards as the subway (and exact cash in coins if you don't have a card). The network of buses is as extensive as the subways, and they run fairly reliably.

CARS

Cabs and cars for hire are great options when you're A) lazy, B) have a lot of stuff, or C) the damn G train ain't comin'. Getting around Brooklyn in a cab, unless you're going from Greenpoint to Coney Island, never runs you more than $20. Now, getting back to Brooklyn from Manhattan, that's a different story. Although it is illegal for drivers not to take you to Brooklyn once you've hailed down a cab, they often continue to refuse service because either it's not cost- and/or time-effective for them or they just have no fucking idea where anything in Brooklyn is.

Green Boro Taxis recently rolled out to service Brooklyn specifically and alleviate the frustration with the anti-BK discrimination of yellow cabs, but they only pick up in the other boroughs; you can't hail one in Manhattan unless you're above 110th Street.

Calling a car service is the old way of doing things, but if you plan a trip ahead of time, most neighborhoods have a car service office nearby. Hailing a cab on a busy street works too. But the best way to get a ride is by using digital-based car services, like Hailo and, more popular, Uber. The cars are clean and prompt, but the cost of comfort is a little higher than regular cabs and fluctuates based on things like rush hour, weather conditions, and holidays.

Zipcar is another car option developed for people who want to make everyday chores and short trips easier. You register with the company and any time you need wheels, Zipcar unlocks an available car (usually within a few blocks from you). You pay by the hour and have the freedom of taking a quick day trip without dealing with public transit. Just return it on time to avoid extra charges.

BIKES

Bikes and Brooklyn go together like peanut butter and jelly. Almost everyone has a bike and uses it daily, even during the colder months. There are extensive bike paths all around Brooklyn, connecting neighborhoods and boroughs (via the bridges). Citi Bikes are a new, locally hated way for people to rent a bike for a short period of time. You just use your credit card to unlock a (big, clunky) bike at their kiosks all around the city. You can bike across both the Brooklyn and Williamsburg Bridges (the Manhattan Bridge is always under construction and the bike path is in disrepair). The Brooklyn Bridge will be a busy tourist experience, with people stepping into the bike lane to take selfies. On the other hand, the grittier Williamsburg Bridge (enter at Roebling and S 4th Street) has a dedicated bike lane and the train rumbles provide a sound track to your ride right into the Lower East Side.

FUN FACT

Brooklynites spend an average of over forty minutes traveling to work every day.

FEET

In Brooklyn, the best form of transportation is undoubtedly your feet. People here walk, and jaywalk, a lot. The city is super-scenic and really easy to navigate on foot.

ACCOMMODATIONS

As you may know, real estate in Brooklyn is tight. Everyone wants to live on this tiny piece of land, which makes for some compromised living situations. You'll find people living in basements, closets, and curtained living room areas, sharing their space with more bodies than the rules of sanity would deem safe. But nobody is here for comfort. Brooklyn is more about boutique hotels and quaint bed-and-breakfasts, which can get pricey. Us broke asses usually stay with friends, but if you don't know anybody in Brooklyn, services like Airbnb, temp listings on Craigslist, and couchsurfing are your best bets for finding a place to drop your bags.

HOSTELS

An abundance of (illegal) hostels used to be available in Brooklyn until the city shut them down. Here are the legit operations that managed to survive the hostelpocalypse.

B Hotel & Hostel
141 Broadway Avenue
$35-$45 per night

A proper dorm-style hostel decorated with that IKEA flair, B Hotel & Hostel has your regular amenities (sheets, WiFi, lockers, etc.) with foosball, Ping-Pong, and pool tables, and huge, brick-walled common areas (including a big-ass kitchen). You'll be close to the J and M trains that will take you to Manhattan in ten to fifteen minutes and within walking distance from central Williamsburg and Bushwick. The neighborhood here is eclectic, with all kinds of divey places to satisfy your cravings for something fast and greasy. If you've never experienced the kind of noise New Yorkers deal with daily, staying here may be a little bit of an ear shock as it's right under the rickety subway and the walls in each room don't fully hit the ceiling.

New York Loft Hostel
249 Varet Street
$50-60 per night

This hostel is in a great part of Bushwick locally known as Morgantown. A straight shot on the L gets you back in the bustle of Manhattan in about fifteen minutes. The meticulously clean, fresh-smelling rooms all have large windows and enough space in them to land a helicopter. There is no doubt that spaciousness is this hostel's best quality, but a close second is its modern, artsy design. All doors (to twelve dorms and about thirty private rooms) and hallways are painted with New York landmarks. The hostel has a pool table, vending machines, fire-escape city views, free breakfast (and other food occasionally), a decent kitchen, and knowledgeable staff.

BED-AND-BREAKFASTS

Less like regular hotels and more like people's homes turned into makeshift hotels, staying at one of these will feel like visiting a relative you don't really speak to.

3B: The Downtown Brooklyn Bed & Breakfast
136 Lawrence Street
Dorms: $50-$65 per night
Rooms: $140-$185 per night

This is the closest you'll get to actually living in Brooklyn without laying down the cash or compromising personal space (and mental sanity) to do so. This place is impeccably decorated and is housed on the third floor of a historical building. It's got all those charming touches you see on home-decorating shows, plus they serve an actual breakfast (with fresh vegetables, baked goods, granola, OJ, coffee, and egg dishes), made every morning from 8:30 to 10:00 a.m. They've got four room options: two double-occupancy private rooms with a queen-size bed (about $140–$155 per night), one room with two separate queen beds (about $170–$185 per night), and a dorm-style room with bunks ($50–$65 per night). You get clean towels and linens, and there are two bathrooms (one with a shower) that are shared by all occupants. The place is right in Downtown Brooklyn and is super close to the Brooklyn Bridge and every subway you'll ever need. The people at 3B are very eco-conscious and friendly, and they strive to keep this place looking fresh and fly.

Greenpoint Lodge
95 Norman Avenue
$35 per night, plus $30–$40 cleaning fee

In the middle of happening Greenpoint, and right next to the Nassau stop, the Greenpoint Lodge is a family home converted into a guest residence. Comprised of several private rooms that will accommodate two to four people, this is an older house, so things will creak and noise will travel. Not a busy hostel packed with backpackers, Greenpoint Lodge is just a place to lay your head in between bar hopping in Williamsburg (ten-minute scenic walk) and brunching in Greenpoint. For $35 per night (plus $30–$40 cleaning fee), you'll get kitchen access to cook up your Saturday farmers' market finds and save cash. It's a nice little option that books up fast during the summer.

AIRBNB

Brooklyn is notorious for unique Airbnb listings. Here you'll find everything from a dinky couch to a full-on artist loft and everything in between. These are some of our favorite recurring listings.

Artist Loft, "Williamsbush"
Bushwick
$65–$90 per night
Airbnb.com/rooms/364275

Filled with inspired clutter, Rico's space is something very unique and he usually has several rooms for rent. The sleeping spaces are small, but you'll get to live inside a huge, eclectic art installation filled with taxidermy, skulls, and weird knickknacks all juxtaposed with colorful sculptures, ornate couches, paintings, and fabrics. The living room is expansive, with a large window to light up all the cool antiques inside. There are six total bedrooms and the roommates come from all walks of life. There's also a cat. Super close to the train in that middle area between Williamsburg and Bushwick, the apartment is inside the popular McKibbin Lofts, a gathering of loft spaces known for their artistic flair and living-out-loud attitude. Things get rowdy, and fun will be had whether you like it or not.

Brooklyn Arts Studio
Fort Greene
$30–$90 per night
Airbnb.com/rooms/289130

Take up temporary residence in an artist's loft to see Brooklyn from an insider's point of view. This unique space is fully decked out in reclaimed wood with access to a remarkable kitchen, bathroom, darkroom, junkyard, and rooftop. There are five rooms available, some with lofted beds, all impeccably decorated. A wacky space infused with creativity in every corner, the artist who lives there uses the space as a studio and aims to share his passion for preserving and reinventing Brooklyn's creative cool with his guests. Near Barclays Center on Dean Street, you're close to all the subways and within walking distance of historical landmarks, famous eateries, and great bars. Since this is a working artist studio, it won't be like a quiet hotel and some rules apply. Depending on the room you book, it'll run you between $30 and $90 per night, with longer stays negotiable.

Note: There may be nudity. The artist who lives here sometimes walks around naked and likes to not worry about it. If you're terrified of nakedness, you can talk to him about it and he'll slap on some pants.

East Williamsburg Loft
Bushwick
$85 per night, plus $20 cleaning fee
Airbnb.com/rooms/1294417

Inside an all-brick, beautifully graffitied building you'll find a clean, wood-accented loft that's tastefully decorated and will make you wish you had better interior design skills. The two rooms for rent here are simple and cozy but give you access to the loft's amenities, which include a rooftop patio with a BBQ area, fireplace, laundry room, an expansive kitchen, fresh coffee, towels, linens, a tree house, and bikes. (Seriously, if you ask nicely, they'll lend you a bike!) The two who call this place home are genuinely nice, and they have a kid and an outdoor cat. The loft is attached to a studio space, is above a bar (the Anchored Inn), and is in a really awesome area (off the L) right near all the action. This means you'll meet local bartenders and musicians and will have to shut up and deal with a bit of noise every now and then.

Private Room
Clinton Hill/Bed-Stuy
$65-$85
Airbnb.com/rooms/453094
Airbnb.com/rooms/42580
Airbnb.com/rooms/31994

This is a serene, rustic spot in a lively neighborhood right near Pratt (Brooklyn's big art school). Here, you've got three options: You can sleep surrounded by brick and windows with access to the garden for $65; a darker, sexier Victorian room on the parlor floor for $70; or the biggest of the three, with an en suite bathroom, private deck, and nonworking ornate fireplace for $85. While there's a minimum two-night stay, these awesome digs will probably lure you in for longer. The apartment is on Lafayette, two blocks from the hated-by-all G train at Clinton-Washington, which will get you around anywhere you'd like to go in Brooklyn pretty quickly (when it's working). Otherwise, this neighborhood offers a lot of fun things within walking distance.

COUCHSURFING

The couchsurfing culture is well established in Brooklyn, and people who offer up their couches tend to be young and eager to show you around town. At any given time, you'll find some great listings, but be warned that during peak tourist seasons (summer; holidays), hosts experience a high volume of requests. If you're planning to take the couch route, plan further in advance than you normally would and contact several hosts to secure a spot. Williamsburg, Bushwick, Greenpoint, and Park Slope are the most popular surfing locations. Consider looking at couches in Bed-Stuy, Gowanus, or Sunset Park instead. These areas will have more availability and are close enough by train to the more popular hoods.

TEMP LISTINGS

Craigslist is a good tool to use if you're planning to stay for more than a couple of days. People pick up and move in this city all the time, which means vacancies in proper apartments can become available last minute. Since the general population here is used to this sort of transience, many places are rented on a month-to-month basis with fully refundable deposits. You'll feel like you actually live in Brooklyn and get to experience it from the grimy ground up.

MONEY

We're all familiar with the U.S. dollar, and in Brooklyn there are still places that only take your paper bills. While most of Brooklyn is down with credit cards, many places (especially bodegas, cafés, and sometimes bars) will usually have a $10 minimum. Packing plastic is great, but make sure to bring a few backup bills for a cup of coffee, a pack of gum, or that one beer to tide you over until lunch. ATMs are all over should you get stuck, and if they're not connected to your bank, you'll be charged a $2-$3 fee for the transaction.

As opposed to the wallet beating you'll get in Manhattan, going out in Brooklyn is reasonable. Many cool shows are free, beers run $5-$7 (on the higher end)—and cocktails are normally under $10. Of course you can always find a place to blow your load, but for the most part, you won't find yourself in the red every night. As for restaurants, Brooklyn is an eclectic mix of cheap and pricey. If all you've got is a Hamilton for dinner, loading up on incredible slices and cheap street food will quiet your broke-ass stomach.

As is true all over the United States, tipping is customary. Throwing your change into a barista's jar, leaving at least 15 percent on your restaurant bill for the waiter, and a few bucks on the cab ride home are all expected. Minimum wage in Brooklyn sucks—don't be a jerk.

HEALTH AND SAFETY

HEALTH

All the regular diseases that plague the rest of the country exist in Brooklyn, plus bed bugs. Scary little fuckers that can live without food for years, bed bugs are always on the mind in Brooklyn. You won't get bitten the minute you step on BK soil, but they aren't entirely an urban legend either. The best thing you can do is avoid sleeping on dirty outdoor furniture, rolling around in dingy sheets, and, if you notice a three-bite pattern (the common breakfast, lunch, and dinner bed-bug bites), get the fuck out of where you are and wash all your clothes in hot water on high.

People in NYC are more packed together and touch things, like subway poles and other public areas, with their grimy little hands. Germs spread easily, so taking a little extra precaution during flu season is necessary. Wash your hands, splurge on some hand sanitizer, and sneeze into your arm to help stop the germs from spreading.

The Gowanus Canal is the dirtiest body of water in all the land. It is full of diseases that would make even the skankiest of college freshmen look like angels. While there are kayaking tours available on that wretched canal, we wouldn't dare touch the poo water and you shouldn't either.

As for things related to your sexy parts—

condoms, lube, tampons, and all that jazz can be purchased at any corner store, market, or bigger convenience store. Should you have an accident, Plan B is now available without a prescription (for relatively cheap) at CVS, Rite Aid, and Duane Reade. Planned Parenthood is also around to offer discounted care to anyone who needs help with their reproductive health. The main office in Downtown Brooklyn (44 Court Street) is clean, the employees there are helpful, and the whole thing costs less than dealing with hospital doctors. If you do need a hospital, the biggest and best is New York Methodist in Park Slope on 7th Avenue and 6th Street.

SAFETY

Brooklyn may have a hard rep, but really, most places are pretty safe unless you're stupid. Crime rates in most neighborhoods have dropped substantially in the last ten years and continue to fall because of funds appropriated to bolster police presence in crackheady neighborhoods. Since many places are open twenty-four hours (or at least late-night) and people are on an around-the-clock schedule, you'll rarely find a dark, empty street in Brooklyn at any hour. As such, you'll always feel a safety in numbers.

None of these rules apply in East New York or Brownsville; these areas are still pretty crime-ridden.

Ladies: Guys will holla at you just because and say hi. Yeah, they're checking you out, but mostly they're just looking to say hello.

Let's talk about weirdos. Brooklyn is home to an incredibly diverse population, culturally, financially, and sanitywise. It may seem that there are way more weirdos in Brooklyn than anywhere else, and while some of that is true, it's also just a product of the way the city is set up. Since life in Brooklyn is lived

in such close quarters, with apartments stuffed to the brim and subways packed like sardine cans, all the crazy makes its way out into the open. Most weirdos are not looking to hurt you in any way. People sing, run, dance, and throw things for no reason. Every now and then somebody will utter a phrase that'll scare the shit out of you (e.g., "I like my puppies medium-rare"). Be conscious of your surroundings and the people who may be lingering in them. If something feels just too shady, you can always pop into a bodega, bar, or other business to shake the weirdo off your path.

CLIMATE

There are four distinct seasons, although some will argue that the fall and spring are way too short. The summers are humid and hot, often reaching temperatures of up to 100 degrees. The winters are brutal, with cold temperatures, rain, and snow starting up around December and not subsiding until late March. The first day of spring in Brooklyn is perhaps the most beautiful day of the year, partly because the weather finally turns brighter and warmer, and mostly because people peel off their winter layers, finally peek their heads outside, and start to dream of the carefree days of summer. Each season has its high points as long as you're dressed appropriately.

OTP Tip: If you're looking for a quick icebreaker with anyone you meet in Brooklyn, the weather is a topic locals discuss (and complain about) daily.

CULTURE AND POLITICS

CULTURE

Diversity

Brooklyn is densely populated and spread out on more land mass than Manhattan. Even though Brooklyn is home to a wide array of cultures, there is a sense of community there that trumps any cultural differences that may exist among its residents. The culture of Brooklyn, as a whole, is defined by the eclectic sum of its parts. Brooklyn has historically been the final destination of many immigrant populations, which have settled in clusters. Brighton Beach is "Little Odessa," but Ukrainians sprawl from Bensonhurst to Coney Island. West Indians run Prospect Heights, and adjacent Crown Heights is all about the Hasidim. Greenpoint is Polish land, Bay Ridge is Italian, and Sunset Park is both Chinese and Mexican. Some of Bushwick is Puerto Rican. The lower rents and bigger living spaces attract generations of families to settle and grow ethnic communities in Brooklyn. They bring their food, customs, language, and traditions. The most interesting thing that happens is the blending of cultures at the borders. Food fuses, fashion is remixed, and new words form. Brooklyn takes much pride in the diversity of its ever-changing population and the innovative, cultural mishmash that emerges from so many different people occupying the same turf.

Brooklyn's LGBT scene is perhaps the most thriving one in the United States. (Step off, San Fran!) People in Brooklyn are very accepting of all kinds of lifestyles and, for the most part, do not judge others based on sexual preferences/identities. The Pride Parade is a highly anticipated, widely attended event for everyone—gay, straight, or whatever. Park Slope is a big gathering of gay, where many couples go to settle down. Nobody really bats an eye at gay PDA. Sure, there's an occasional jerk who doesn't get it, but the sexual politics here are mostly open, free, and accepting.

Art

Brooklyn has a thriving art culture. Since the high standard of living in the LES has actually starved a few artists, the classic hoboesque lifestyle has been transported across the river. More than just incubating museum-worthy artists and being home to the Pratt Institute (a world-renowned art school), Brooklyn is famous for pumping out street artists by the gaggles. As seen on just about any wall in the city, Brooklyn's street artists are insanely creative, constantly putting up fresh work, and figuring out new ways to keep the streets vibrant with art. Galleries all over Bushwick exhibit artists working in the hood, and cafés across Brooklyn put up new shows monthly to display the works of Brooklyn's abundant local talent.

Food

Brooklyn residents are die-hard when it comes to their favorite eateries, food trucks, and specialty stores. Brooklyn's food culture is focused on locally made and sourced goods, crafted to perfection by people who give a big ol' damn about pleasing the palates of discerning residents. In Brooklyn, you'll find the best version of everything you can dream up: hibiscus doughnuts at Dough; perfectly pickled cukes at McClure's; lobster rolls so buttery you'll feel your heart flip at Red Hook Lobster Pound; and chocolate fit for (bearded) kings at Mast Brothers. Brooklyn does pizza right (old-school and new), they've got bagels on lock, and if you want to taste a little of everything, all at once, Smorgasburg pops up in various locations on the weekends to bring you the best of local flavors.

Music

The music culture in Brooklyn is on par with its art scene. Just about everyone there is in a band or can at least sing well enough without ripping your ears apart. Popping down into the subway for a few stops (especially at the Lorimer Street / Metropolitan Avenue L/G interchange) will expose you to the caliber of musical talent this borough has to offer. Sure, there are open mikes and legit signed bands around town, but the raw talent you hear down there, from the solo guitar-playing singer to the cross-platform rap battle/power ballad duo is unbelievable.

POLITICS

Brooklyn as a whole is liberal and outspoken. When something needs changing, there is always a group in place to rally up angry residents. That's how historic buildings get preserved when faced with land-hungry condo developers. When something sounds shady, Brooklynites protest on the streets.

The race and income politics in Brooklyn these days look a little different than they did during Spike Jonze's Brooklyn of the '80s and '90s. Gentrification is not a new word or phenomenon, but it is the best way to describe the source of tension felt across various Brooklyn communities. The high rents of Manhattan apartments push young professionals (yuppies) to move to certain parts of Brooklyn, which displaces old-time residents to make way for people who can afford a higher standard of living. New yuppie businesses spring up in response and

many poorer residents are "priced out" of the neighborhoods they grew up in. The politics here are very delicate. While some people think that everyone should be able to afford to stay in their childhood homes, at the same time, others believe that gentrification brings economic development to neighborhoods. No matter what side of the argument you find yourself on, this is a hot topic in the politics of Brooklyn, so being aware of it is very important when you visit.

FASHION

The key to Brooklyn fashion is to look like you don't give a fuck while secretly really giving a fuck. And it's all in the shoes. It's OK to look beat up from head to ankles, but when you glance down at people's shoes on the subway, you'll see nothing but style. Brooklynites despise Uggs and flip-flops and will go the extra mile of bringing back-up

flats for rougher terrain so that they can sport that sassy pair once they arrive at their destination. First impressions, business decisions, and attractiveness are ascertained with a quick glance down below. Wear nice shoes if you want to fuck.

From the feet up, Brooklyn has an eclectic sense of style. While Manhattanites button up during the day, Brooklyn's more creative professional population has the liberty to break out of the monkey suit, and they do it with flair. On any given workday, you'll see worklike outfits paired with bold jewelry, cool old-timey hats and vests, and worn-in jeans.

For the most part, people stay away from the mainstream H&M and Forever 21. With access to limitless vintage and secondhand clothing shops like Buffalo Exchange and Beacon's Closet; one-of-a-kind, locally made wares from the Brooklyn Flea; and various street/stoop sales, it makes sense that

Brooklynites take pride in crafting eclectic outfits, and they can do it on a dime.

At night, well that's when the "weirder is better" mantra holds truest. During the hot and humid summers, party-wear is skimpy yet stylish. The idea is to wear as little as possible but still give off an air of Brooklyn chic, and the women of Brooklyn are masters of the side-boob and under-butt. The winter nightscape is a little different. While people still dress a little slutty, they are fully aware of the biting cold that'll freeze their hoo-ha straight off if they don't cover up, so plush winter coats make their way out with the heels and short skirts.

It isn't a myth that New Yorkers wear a lot of black. Black is easy, and in a place where life is sometimes hard, it makes sense to just throw on something stylish that doesn't require much fuss.

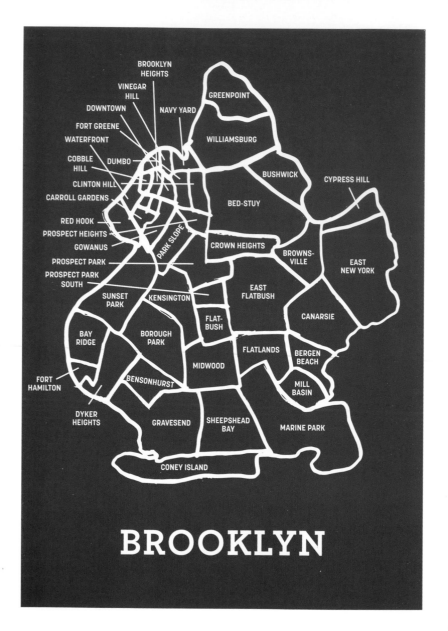

BROOKLYN

NEIGHBORHOODS

Manhattan's cheaper, cooler (actually older) brother, Brooklyn is where America's collection of internationals mash together into a steaming stew of culture. A great place to lose your backpacking virginity, this borough will take you around the world with every train stop: Dominican/Pakistani bodegas and West African restaurants in Notorious B.I.G.'s Bed-Stuy, hipster kingdoms in Williamsburg and Bushwick, all things Italian in Bay Ridge, Polish peeps in Greenpoint, and Ukraine's home away from home in Brighton Beach. Like biting into a cross-section of the world, Brooklyn lives in layers of nationalities, piled high on top of each other in historic brownstones. You want a side of pierogi with your calzone? Brooklyn's got you, boss.

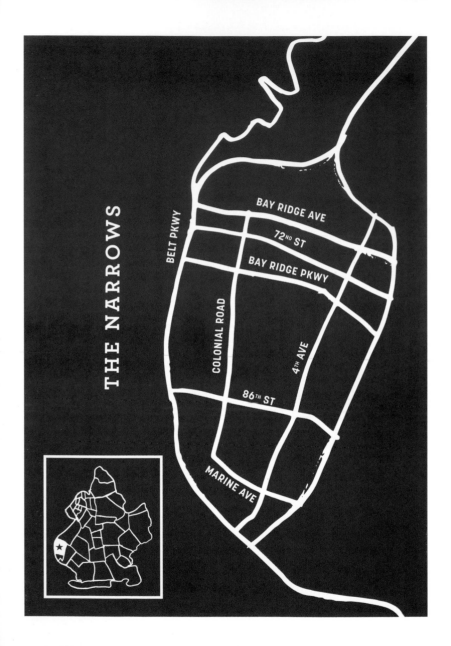

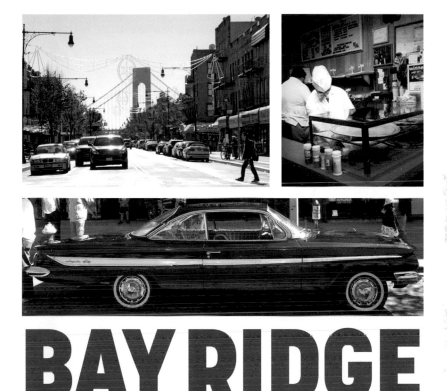

BAY RIDGE

If you're looking for an earful of fuggetaboutit, this is guido
paradise. Sure, a lot of Bay Ridge is composed of families just
looking to get away from the bustle, but it is where the basil
and ricotta flavors are most prominent. Most restaurants
here don't fuck around with nouveau Italian. They don't put
kale in your calzones or Korean short ribs on your pizza. In
Bay Ridge, tradition is what matters most. If you ever find a
hair in your cannoli here, it will likely be gray and belong to
an old nonna.

COFFEE AND BAKERIES

OMONIA CAFE
#dessert #cheesecake
7612 3rd Avenue

The décor at this place is super weird, with booths that look like they're cut out of stacks of pancakes and an outdoor space that feels like a makeshift Miami nightclub. But you may not even notice the nutty designs because your face will be drawn to the dessert display and will remain there until you realize they have baklava cheesecake. This cake is mighty special. The flakey, honey-soaked pastry stands in for the crust and surrounds a perfectly creamy cheesecake. Feel free to pursue other offerings, but trust us, this Mid-East-meets-Brooklyn cake is what'll turn you rabid with every forkful.

ROBICELLI'S
#bakery #cupcakes
9009 5th Avenue

The cupcake craze was a ridiculous food epidemic, and, if our calculations are correct, coincided with the popularity of jeggings (the stretchy, wannabe pants for those who can't figure out how to squeeze themselves into denim). While many a bakery cupcaked and failed, Robicelli's continues to withstand the test of time. This is a husband-and-wife operation, and both are completely dedicated to shocking you with the weird shit they can make into a cupcake. With a rotation of more than 250 wacky flavors, these dudes are still busy remastering the cupcake and don't care if everyone else has moved on to doughnuts.

THE COFFEE LAB
#espresso #ScienceOfCoffee
6903 3rd Avenue

When trekking to Bay Ridge kills your caffeine buzz, the Coffee Lab is a legit coffee shop dedicated to perking your ass back into business. A wide-open, clean space, the baristas are mad coffee scientists and the décor is streamlined but not sterile. They serve pastries from Balthazar and their beans come from Williamsburg roaster, Toby's Estate. Get something with espresso and feel human again.

 **EAT**

GINO'S RESTAURANT
#OldSchool #Italian
7414 5th Avenue

Going to Bay Ridge means hitting a good Italian spot, and Gino's has been around for more than fifty years, serving its dishes to the authenticity-seeking masses. You can taste the nonna love in their slow-cooked sauces, the pasta is always made right, and the chicken Parm may back up an artery but hot damn it's good! They serve hearty Italian portions but manage to keep the presentations neat and blob-free.

FUN FACT

Saturday Night Fever was filmed in Bay Ridge.

HO'BRAH: A TACO JOINT
#GringoTacos
8618 3rd Avenue

If the name doesn't tip you off, brah, this place is all about Cali Mexican, and they do it so right. Each one of their corn-tortilla-cradled tacos is a masterpiece in West Coast flavor. They've got the fish taco nailed, with perfectly fried cod chunks, slaw, cheese, salsa, punchy lime, and sour cream falling from every corner of that tortilla. They throw in chipotle (and bourbon!) into the charred steak taco, and if you get it with pickled jalapeños and a side of guac, you'll start feeling the warm Cali breeze hitting your face with every bite. Ho'Brah gets their fish from the nearby market on 87th Street and 3rd Avenue, pairs it with bold flavors, and serves it up in a surf atmosphere decked out with boards.

TACO T...

Complaints that New York City is devoid of authentic Mexican food can stop right here. Nearby Sunset Park has a huge Mexican population that concocts the spiciest, guaca-moliest, down-right taco burritoiest eats in all of NYC, and at a price fit for the homey food it's supposed to be. These are the Mexican spots we hold dearest to our hearts.

TACOS EL BRONCO
4324 4th Avenue

West Coasters rave about this place being on point, and we agree; El Bronco aces their tacos. The pickings are way more delicious than their cobbled-together Microsoft Office menu may suggest. Their carne al pastor, spit-charred and wonderful, is the tits. They've got your usual suspects (steak, chicken, and pork, etc.), but kick it up a notch with some interesting meats like *lengua* (tongue), *tripa* (tripe, or stomach lining), and *cabeza* (veal head). They've also got two trucks on the road in the area if taking your tacos for a walk is the plan.

TAQUERIA EL MAGUEY
3910 4th Avenue

The carne asada in this joint is so tender and juicy it'll never end up stuck in your teeth cracks. A hole in the wall, Maguey has a large following for its awesome tacos, tamales, and other authentic dishes. It's a space that's always jam-packed, mostly with real Mexicans—because it's real Mexican food. The all-green décor accentuates the freshness of its offerings.

TACOS LOS POBLANOS
5320 5th Avenue

Things are about to get real messy! This food stand is packed with guys busily making tacos to order. They're doing God's taco work in a small space that pumps out huge flavors. The tacos are cheap, and you get to sauce them with squeeze bottles of either red or green salsa. Here's the trick: Get five tacos and they'll throw in a whole grilled onion. Proceed to sauce those little love pouches with enough salsa verde to turn your elbow into a green juice faucet.

TACOS MATAMOROS
4508 5th Avenue

A cultish taco destination, you'll find that Matamoros doesn't mess around when it comes to tacos. When regular tacos won't do, Matamoros brings out the big guns with their supersized beastly tacos, stuffed so full that they need paper wrappers to hold it all together. (And still under $5!) There's something magical about their salsa verde, their guac has the cilantro-lime ratio right, and the chorizo is well spiced. Despite all the gringos you'll see inside, Matamoros is authentic Mexican right down to the carne asada. There's a second location down the street, but stick to the OG for your fix of flavor.

TACO STAND
corner of 60th Street and 4th Avenue

Walking by, you will be drawn in by the smell of tacos wafting around the stand, especially late at night (the guy's there until 6:00 a.m.!) when you're swaying from side to side on a frantic search for something awesome. All the meat is grilled right there, and the beef and chicken are solid. Get yourself a pair and sauce up those bitches any way you like.

HOM
#brunch #quirky
8806 3rd Avenue

You'll walk in and wonder why we sent you somewhere to browse lamps and odd knick-knacks. Be patient, friend. The storefront is a vintage furnishings boutique and the back is all about brunch. Drop Grandma off at the doilies and trinkets while you go get green eggs and ham (and sangria at noon). The café's menu changes frequently, but you can always depend on brunch regulars like eggs, bacon, pancakes, baked goods, sandwiches, and homemade jams. The portions are satisfying, and the servers know you're likely hungover, so they use their inside voices.

MIKE'S HINSCH GREEK AMERICAN DINER
#OldSchool #diner #DrunkFood
8518 5th Avenue

Hinsch's has been a Bay Ridge staple for decades and is famous for the type of midnight munchies that old Brooklynites love best. Come here for late-night egg creams and floats, or roll out of bed whenever for some kick-ass pancakes, omelets, sandwiches, and crispy sweet potato fries. The service is super-friendly, and it's the kind of place you'll wish was around the corner when you were skipping school. Greek food? Yeah, they've got that too. It was recently overtaken by another (real estate tycoon) Mike, but he knows better than to change anything about this legendary spot.

PIZZA WAGON
#OldSchool #pizza
8610 5th Avenue

We're not sure that pizzas and wagons have any business being strung together, but this is a classic neighborhood pizza joint and the pies will hit the spot every time. The atmosphere is of your typical pizza joint with stand-up tables, so you can stretch out your intestines while gobbling up slice after slice. The slices come in triangles or squares (corners!) with fresh melty cheese, tangy sauce, and a crunchy crust. For $4 you can get a slice and a soda and leave the place feeling like you've done it right. Roll on, little pizza wagon, and spread your good pizza cheer.

TANOREEN
#FoodNetwork #TreatYourself #MiddleEastern
7523 3rd Avenue

Tanoreen is a small operation that made it big-time, with Food Network attention and all. The talk on the TV was all about their *knafeh*, a phyllo dessert that's cheesy and nutty. But there is so much more amazing food to be found here. Aside from sweets, Tanoreen is a stand-out on the huge NYC Middle Eastern scene. Not your thrown-together falafel joint, chef/owner Rawia Bishara creates inspired, slow-cooked, well-spiced dishes that she learned from her innovative mother. The menu is lamb-heavy, but the variety of preparations, sides, and spices makes for a different mouthful with every dish. If you do it right, you won't have room for dessert . . . but you should probably get it anyway.

◉ SEE AND DO

69TH STREET PIER (AMERICAN VETERAN'S MEMORIAL PIER)

#view #bike

Shore Road and Bay Ridge Avenue

A waterfront not overrun by tourists, come here to stare into the NYC distance and enjoy some gorgeous sunsets. You can gaze at the famous skyline from a new angle, with a little Verrazano Bridge in the background. In the summer of 2012, the pier got a $1.1 million eco dock addition that often holds free educational seminars about NYC waterways and gives boat tours. If your sneakers get itchy, you can join the locals for a run or bike ride along the promenade. If you have zero interest in breaking a sweat, sit back with a blunt and watch people fish and be merry.

SHOP

CENTURY 21
#deals #clothes #shoes
472 86th Street

Everyone knows about the Manhattan location of this famous NYC discount store, but the Bay Ridge branch is far superior. No wide-eyed tourists here pawing through everything and clogging the aisles. This Century 21 is all about boss swagger on the cheap. Their overflowing merchandise is housed in two stores, with the shoe heaven shop across the street. Perfect for brand whores and couldn't-give-a-shit shoppers, this Century 21 has all the right threads.

HIT CHINATOWN WITH CONFIDENCE

The largest in New York, Brooklyn's take on stateside China is an enjoyably confusing stretch of Pan-Asian paradise that spans about twenty blocks. On the street, you'll see piles of produce, still-moving seafood, a wide selection of noodle houses, dim sum, and enough socks to last you for eternity. More than China is represented here; it's a cross-section of culture that includes offerings from Malaysia, Korea, Vietnam, and Thailand. Hop off the N train at 8th Avenue and don't be afraid of the unfamiliar street signs and food hanging out on the sidewalks.

😊 **PARTYING**

LOCK YARD
#BeerGarden #backyard
9221 5th Avenue

Lock Yard is a beer garden with craft beers, a banging backyard, and a huge selection of artisanal sausages (with wild toppings)—plus fried pickles. They don't have a full bar, but you won't care. Their beer menu rotates weekly and they know that yard is a gem, so they keep it heated and beautifully lit to stretch the most out of al fresco season.

THE OWL'S HEAD
#WineBar #oysters
479 74th Street

A cool, new wine bar without a drop of wino pretension, the food is equally good, and the area allows wine prices to stay affordable. But just because it's cheap doesn't mean it's not über fancy. The bar is made from a single maple tree, the place is wrapped in exposed brick, and the charcuterie (cheese and meat plates, people!) are carefully selected and sourced locally from cheese aficionados, Stinky Bklyn. They also throw a great $1 oyster night.

SALTY DOG
#SportsBar #DrunkDancing
7509 3rd Avenue

How do you make a sports bar better? Mix in a little firehouse flare. This old firehouse is a sports bar that gets super rowdy late at night. It's divey but has an old-school neighborhood feel; everyone is always drunk and eating something greasy. You'll come in here for a beer, things will quickly escalate into dancing on tables, and, unavoidably, the night will turn wild and you'll find yourself passed out near the vintage fire truck. We dare you to just have a quiet, sit-down conversation. Ain't gonna happen, boss.

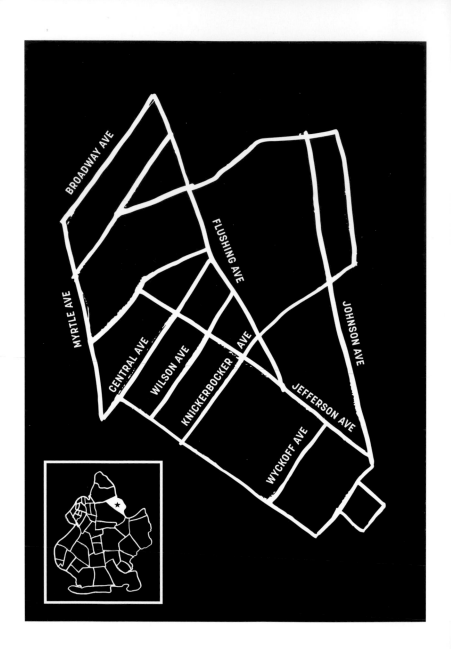

BROADWAY AVE

FLUSHING AVE

MYRTLE AVE

JOHNSON AVE

CENTRAL AVE

WILSON AVE

KNICKERBOCKER AVE

JEFFERSON AVE

WYCKOFF AVE

BUSHWICK

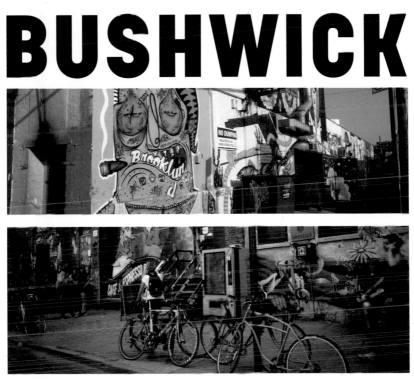

Mostly made up of industrial lofts, Bushwick is like Williamsburg's just-as-weird, but different, little brother. Since there is more room to move around (and make cool shit) than in Williamsburg, the lofts in Bushwick house a lot of creative people. Get off at any L stop in Bushwick and you'll be face-raped by all kinds of graffiti and bands practicing their latest electro-pop/grunge/hip-hop combo jams. Bushwick's vintage stores are the real, mothball-smelly deal; the loft parties never reach capacity; and the many cafés all brew the brown strong to keep you amped until something pops. Anything goes here, and there is never a curfew.

COFFEE AND BAKERIES

ANGE NOIR CAFÉ
#coffee #lunch #LiveMusic #French
247 Varet Street

Owned by a not-snotty French couple, Ange Noir is a quirky place that isn't trying too hard to be French but is dotted with enough Frenchiness to give it an interesting vibe. The coffee here is Stumptown, and the atmosphere is as if France and Brooklyn ran into each other at a high enough speed to combine décor forces. Flanked by brick, there are little lamps on the tables and the restroom door is housed inside a telephone booth. A nice place to set up for a few hours of work, Ange Noir is both chic and comfortable and never that crowded. They've got quiche and croissants, but if you get hungry, the sandwiches (with cheesy international country names) are absolutely amazing. If you're staying at the Loft Hostel, make this your morning breakfast joint. They also hold live music performances for locals at 8:00 p.m. on Thursdays (at which point it gets a little loud and sometimes obnoxious).

CAFETERIA LA MEJOR
#coffee #MiamiCuban
191 Suydam Street

A little bit of Miami's Cuban fusion flavor in Bushwick, La Mejor serves up coffee and a small selection of well-made sandwiches in a bright-blue-and-neon-pink-accented shop. La Mejor is less like Miami threw up on Brooklyn and more of a tasteful approach to the loud, vibrant vibe. Their coffee isn't typical of your average coffee shop; their focus is mixing your coffee perfectly with milk to create *cortaditos* or serving it up with milk, sugar, a pinch of salt, and a bit of butter. (That's right, fucking butter!) They're got the Cuban (both meat and veg), but the Meridian, with its ham, Swiss, and hot pepper guava jelly, is something Miami dreams are made of. Stroll up to the bright take-out window on a nice day, get yourself a Miami breakfast, and drift away to a world of silicone-stuffed bikinis and burnt-caramel tans.

CENTRAL CAFE
#coffee #breakfast
108 Central Avenue

A tiny, cozy, brick-and-wood café, Central is a perfect neighborhood shop, with seating set up like a living room, and old books and pinecones lining the windowsill. The coffee here is Intelligentsia and a little pricier than most, but if you bring in your own mug, they knock down your drink by twenty-five cents. The spot is perfect for breakfast, with sandwiches named after big streets in the neighborhood (like the Jefferson), bagels with a variety of spreads, and a few pastries. The baristas are short and to the point; they don't smile, and there's no bullshit small talk—the kind of people you need to see in the morning when you don't feel like carrying on a conversation about the weather.

DUN-WELL DOUGHNUTS
#doughnuts #vegan #FoodNetwork
222 Montrose Avenue

When you're sitting on the L train under somebody's unkempt armpit, and a doughnut craving strikes, hop off at the Montrose stop and sweet, fluffy, unique rounds of dough are waiting to sop up your saliva. The décor here is Old English, and the doughnut recipes are cruelty-free nuevo chic, as all those colorful doughnuts are completely vegan. Dun-Well doesn't just go a step beyond cardboard but blows conventional 'nuts out of the water with their tender (sans) buttery creations. On any given day, the shop sells a wide variety of creative and classic doughnuts. From their Boston cream to the jelly-stuffed PB&J, Dun-Well pumps out newsworthy doughnuts that have landed them on "best of" lists almost immediately since their opening in 2011. They've also got great Brooklyn Roasting Company coffee to help wash down all that compassion.

KÁVÉ
#lattes #CoolVibes
123 Knickerbocker Avenue

Kávé is the busy coffee shop throbbing at the center of Shops at the Loom, a Bushwick-style mini-mall with crafty goods, art spaces, a yoga studio, tattoo shop, vintage store,

and other small businesses. Reminiscent of a rum-soaked den somewhere in Cuba, Kávé is decked out in wood, metal, and wicker. They offer your standard coffee drinks but up the ante with flavored lattes like mint, coconut, and maple (which can be made with nut milks). Their sandwiches are also pretty damn tasty. The bathroom situation here is confusing, with stalls seamlessly incorporated into a tall metallic inset by the entrance. But once you figure it out, you're golden. Since Kávé (the Hungarian word for "coffee") is a little hidden, you always feel like you're safe from whatever weirdness may be lurking outside.

LULA BEAN CAFE
#coffee #cookies #European
797 Grand Street

Get off the L train at Grand, don't you even dare look at Dunkin' Donuts, and pop into Lula Bean about a half block down. The maximum amount of cute the cool kids can tolerate, Lula is a small shop with only five little bistro tables, benches make up most of the seating. The slightly sleepy baristas serve Segafredo coffee, an Italian roaster unheard of in Brooklyn. If you've been to Italy, you'll remember the name from the little stick-shaped sugar packets served with your espresso abroad (which they've got here too!). Lula also serves paninis, muffins (from our favorite Blue Sky Bakery), bagels, and other light breakfast and lunch stuff common to most café menus, plus homemade pie.

SWALLOW
#coffee #grungy
49 Bogart Street

Right off the Morgan Avenue L stop and in the middle of the busiest corner in Bushwick (aka Morgantown), no matter the time or weather, it always feels like a balmy sunset inside of Swallow. You walk up a few metal steps to get in and walk across creaky floorboards to get to the counter, where they brew Brooklyn Roasting Company beans, sometimes with a smile, sometimes with a sideways smirk. All of the chairs and tables are a little bit wobbly, and the windows let in an odd glow. In order to get to the bathroom, you have to go out into the internal hallway of the building and around the corner. From the smells to the sounds, everything is quirky about this place, but when you're not feeling particularly put-together, it's comforting to pop into a place that seems to be lacking some polish itself.

THE COBRA CLUB
#coffee #bar #quirky
6 Wyckoff Avenue

This is like a rec center where you can fulfill all your vices at once. It's a coffee shop, yoga studio, sports bar, pool hall, booze hole, and event space. This place is like a grimy dive bar in its infantile stages, where things are still conspicuously new and the seats, normally dedicated to ancient regulars sipping brewskies at 10:00 a.m., have yet to be filled. Even the bathroom has a "clean for now" feel with only a bit of graffiti and acceptable funk levels. Catering to the old-men hearts of young Bushwick hipsters, the coffee part of Cobra slings Dough doughnuts and brews Counter Culture beans (at a bodega-low $1.50 for a small drip!). The bar part of Cobra has a big projector screen that blows up come game day, a decent pool table in the back, and a full bar with a great selection of beers on tap. You can come here with a laptop, to hair-of-the-dog your hangover, to do yoga, play pool, watch the game, sing off-key on karaoke nights, and watch your life pass you by without a care in the world.

VARIETY
#coffee #coffice
368 Graham Avenue

The inside feels a bit French, with strategically placed panels of flower wallpaper, but without all the fancy frills that make you crave quiche. They serve Stumptown, and the baristas really know how to keep their shit together (with a smile even) when there's a line out the door. The space is big enough for setting up shop for the day (although their Internet is spotty), with a large communal table up front that lets you glance away from your screen and out onto Graham Avenue.

 # EAT

BUNNA CAFE
#dinner #communal #Ethiopian #vegan
1084 Flushing Avenue

Bunna started as a floating, pop-up (vegan) Ethiopian restaurant that conducted elaborate coffee ceremonies wherever they called home for the night. Don't let the vegan part trip you up; while their dishes might be comprised of just vegetables, beans, and spices, the flavors here are complex. You order based on how hungry you are, choosing the number of items you want on your platter. The options change regularly but you can always bet on the *misir wat* (slow-cooked red lentils with spicy berbere), *keysir* (perfectly roasted beets, carrots, and potatoes), and *gomen* (steamed kale with carrots). You get little mounds of the dishes you order on top of a fresh, pliable piece of *injera* (a sour Ethiopian pancake) with another piece on the side to use in lieu of utensils. Once you're done swirling your little mounds, you get a wet nap and a smile. If you don't feel like chewing, they have these thick purée layered juices (with mango, avocado, and papaya, blended with grenadine, then stacked) that'll act as a hearty liquid stand-in for lunch. For everything to be truly *eshi*, down some honey wine and don't miss their authentic coffee ceremony where a lady prepares the strong brew over coals.

CAFÉ GHIA
#brunch #dinner #cozy
24 Irving Avenue

We love that the owners of this welcome addition to Bushwick's Restaurant Row kept the old "Family Restaurant" sign out front, but don't let the chipping paint and rusted tin fool you. If you're looking for one of the best brunches off the island, this joint gives any Williamsburg stronghold a run for its money. Seasonal drinks and sides that change daily give Ghia a transient feel, and cozy dining quarters are offset with windowed walls and an airy pass-through to the kitchen. Food is Brooklyn Americana, and highlights include the pulled-pork sandwich for dinner, braised in a Brooklyn microbrew, and the veg-friendly biscuits-and-mushroom gravy (sub bacon if you're a carnivore) for breakfast.

DILLINGER'S
#lunch #ModernRussian
146 Evergreen Street

Old-recipe comfort dishes sold in dingy Brighton Beach restaurants are great, but Russian food has been in need of a remix, and the ladies at this out-of-the-way café have done it justice. While messing with a good thing might be sacrilege in the eyes of America's large Russian population (perhaps the reason this café opened as far away from the Russkies as possible), Dillinger's serves up things like borscht, pelmeni, and golubtsy with tiny twists that make a big difference. The pelmeni are pillowy soft, stuffed with your choice of meat or potatoes and mushrooms, and come sprinkled with a Japanese citrusy red pepper for a little kick and tang. The whole place has a homey yet modern feel with a honeycomb wall separator at the entrance, a mosaic lining one wall, and Russian kettles decorating the shelves behind the counter.

FALANSAI
#dinner #ModernVietnamese
112 Harrison Place

A super-clean but not sterile Vietnamese restaurant, walking into this place feels like you just took a nice cold shower. No clutter, simple lighting, and a little bit of pastel blue paint is all the décor Falansai needs. The food here shines against such a minimalist backdrop. You'll find classic and quirky Vietnamese flavors here. The shrimp and okra, catfish clay pot, pumpkin curry, and shaking beef (with filet mignon up in that bitch) are saucy standout dishes and served with rice. It may be weird to order a French dessert here, but get the chestnut mille crêpe cake, with twenty thin crêpe layers doused in pastry cream and served with bourbon sauce. It seems like they're still working on getting their lunchtime pho right, so come here for dinner and enjoy the chill vibes.

MOMINETTE
#lunch #French
221 Knickerbocker Avenue

Forget snooty Frenchmen who smell like BO and cigarettes—if you're craving a little ooh la la, look no further than this classic French bistro with a Bushwick twist. Yes, your waiter will have dreads or a handlebar 'stache, but the croque madame is slobbery-good, and there are enough classic French touches—like antique mirrors so you can slyly check out the hottie reading Sartre two tables down—to make it feel like the Champs-Élysées. Visit in the warm weather and take advantage of the *très jolie* garden out back. With flowers curling from overhead trellises, wrought-iron patio tables, and a communal seating option, you'd swear you were dining in a fancy French vineyard.

MOMO SUSHI SHACK
#dinner #BrokeFancy #Japanese
43 Bogart Street

Given the grunge factor of the surrounding neighborhood, it's hard to wrap your mind around the freshness of the fish at Momo. A little shack mixed into the busy Morgantown block of the sidewalk right off the L, Momo serves up some of the best, most creative sushi in Brooklyn. Behind the shack's doors, you'll enter a paradise of fish (and then some), where seats are comprised of communal tables and the lighting is dim. Get the Party Bomb, a sampling of their balled-up tuna, salmon, and eel, to give you a good idea of what you've gotten yourself into. To steer away from sea life, try the Pork Betty, a super-juicy pork belly swimming in sake and best eaten with a farm-fresh egg, or switch gears and go vegan with the tofu salad (which only sounds boring).

ROBERTA'S
#pizza #FamousFood
261 Moore Street

Whenever anything gets popular in this town, the naysayers accumulate. Sure, the place is crawling with hipsters and looks like a rundown shack, but Roberta's is busy for a reason. Everything on the menu, from the fried Brussels sprouts to the mouth-punching pizzas, is absolutely, ridiculously delicious. Named after the co-owner's mom, this place isn't quite your Italian parents' kitchen. Everything gets gussied up with fresher than fresh ingredients from their rooftop garden, ironic names, and a whole lot of innovation from their super-creative chefs. Their menu is printed daily, and our favorite regular on the menu is "the Bee Sting," a pizza that hits you with something salty (sopressata), spicy (chili), and sweet (honey), on top of the crispy tomato-and-mozz-topped crust in perfect harmony. Roberta's has a radio station in the back and is also known for throwing some weird-ass parties (e.g., their weed-spiced theme party in the summer of 2012, when marijuana pesto was generously drizzled over the specially prepared menu items).

TORTILLERIA MEXICANA LOS HERMANOS
#tacos #FreshTortillas #cheap
271 Starr Street

Perhaps all the complaints about Mexican food on the East Coast being bland didn't come from the lack of seasoning, as originally thought, but rather laid in the freshness of the tortilla. At Hermanos, tortillas just don't get any fresher. A tortilla factory first, Hermanos slings simple Mexican food but wraps it in right-off-the-press tortillas. This place has a cult following and for good reason. Their carnitas and steak tacos are overstuffed and consistently rock, the prices are super-low, and the ladies behind the counter look like they mean Mexican business.

WAFFLE & WOLF
#lunch #sandwiches
413 Graham Avenue

We've surpassed the bread as a vehicle for sandwich fillings, with things like crispy chicken skins and flattened plantains taking on the heavy lifting. Here, the waffle steps in to bring some unique flavors from your hands to your mouth. You can go the sweet or savory, sandwich or stack, route here, with either a regular cornbread (gluten-free) or one made from buckwheat waffle (which happens to be both vegan and gluten-free). From tender pulled pork to pumpkin-pie spread to their excellent house-made tomato jam, their fillings are absolutely amazing. The most popular thing here is #12, an out-of-order item on the menu that's got everything lined-up just right. Bacon is baked right into your waffle, then filled with cheddar, tomato, arugula for bite, and a creamy avocado yogurt. No longer a breakfast-only option, waffles just got a promotion to lunch, dinner, and beyond.

SEE AND DO

BUSHWICK OPEN STUDIOS
#LocalArtSuperExhibit #music #food

Every summer, unique spaces in Bushwick open up to multimedia artists and showcase everything from paintings to wild performances. During this neighborhood-wide festival, lofts, cafés, warehouses, restaurants, bars, and residential lobbies connect with local artists to put on a two-day show like no other. Once everything is set, maps are made of the venues and people can walk for hours during the fest, through the mind-blowing installations and performances, food and drink stalls, and music-filled streets, stopping into the random nooks and crannies of Bushwick to view the work of the latest creatives coming out of the neighborhood.

GET FAT BROOKLYN
#FancyShop #AnnieLloyd
405 Humboldt Street

We're proud to say that Annie Lloyd, the owner of this amazing, high-end shop, has imbedded some ink onto OTP's shoulders back when she worked at Three Kings. We may have a little personal bias toward the artist, but she really is quite talented. Get Fat is Annie's own shop, and it's really comfortable and classy. The wait list here is long, and the prices reflect her popularity. Her ink lines are super-clean, her designs are wacky and beautiful, and she's got a good touch and pleasant attitude.

GOOSE TATTOO
#LegendaryArtists #creative
163 Montrose Avenue

The owner here, Nalla Smith, is a San Francisco tattoo legend who worked at Tattoo City, Ed Hardy's tattoo shop, before the douche-baggery days of being able to wear shirts with tats instead of making a fucking lifelong commitment. His own shop has nothing to do with tats on sneakers and a lot to do with bringing you a quality, welcoming tat session backed by a ton of experience, creativity, and know-how. Given his talent and notoriety, Nalla's rates are reasonable ($200/hour), and if you can't book with the man himself, Pov (John Poverty, formerly of popular LES shop Thicker Than Water) can take care of your tattoo needs too.

JUICY ART FESTIVAL
#StreetArt #InternationalSuperstars

A newcomer to the fest scene, Juicy is a massive street art show that takes over entire blocks of industrial buildings in Bushwick for three days in June. Artists from all over the world gather to paint the available walls, musicians provide tunes to get the creativity flowing, and people come to view the works in progress. Admission is $8-$10, and even if you can't make it out for the festival, visiting the sites postfest will give you a look at some of the freshest street art in Brooklyn.

PUERTO RICAN DAY PARADE
#LoudMusic #MassiveBlockParty
271 Starr Street

A loud, ass-shaking parade that blares sweet salsa sounds along the streets of Williamsburg, this parade celebrates the vibrant culture of Puerto Rico in all its glory. Sure, there is a big-brother version in Manhattan that runs along 5th Avenue, but this parade is more homey. Going strong for more than thirty years, the parade route runs through the Brooklyn streets that Puerto Rican residents call home (mainly Graham Avenue, aka "Avenue of Puerto Rico"), which creates a special block-party feel.

STREET ART WALK

While the losers in Manhattan are craning their heads to get a glimpse of some art, the streets of Brooklyn are pumping out eye-level visuals all over Bushwick and beyond. Festivals like Bushwick Open Studios and Juicy Art Fest, along with art groups like Brooklyn Collective, promote the creation of large-scale, lasting street art. You'll see famous scribbles, newcomers, and some funny random shit along the way.

Note: This walk is just a suggested route. Make random right turns, hop off the train a few stops early, and you'll likely come up on some cool art all on your own.

BEDFORD STOP

Start at 10th Street and Driggs

One of the first things to catch your eye will be Colonel Sander's head superimposed on a chicken followed by Veng RWK's stork. Nearby, you'll see popular Iranian artists' mural "Dream" next to some inspirational quotes interspersed among the art and brick.

There's also a large note written on a garage door in red paint that explains (presumably to the ugly condo residents across the street) that music is supposed to be played loud.

Once you hit Union, swing a right and keep your eyes peeled for ROA's animal pile-up piece (corner of North 9th Street and Havemeyer Street). The Belgian artist is famous for his sketchbook-like beasts. This one's a skunk, raccoon, and fox stack.

MORGAN(TOWN) STOP

Start at Morgan Avenue and Bogart Street

Take a right and watch your elbows. You'll be thrown onto a large pedestrian throughway, with several blocks of insane art. Hang a left at Grattan Street and check out the wall Pixel Pancho did in front of Pinebox Rockshop.

MORGANTOWN & BEYOND

Jump back onto Bogart and head toward Flushing, stopping off at Varet for another Pixel Pancho piece on the side of Tutu's. Entitled "Where's My Whale?" this piece is a nod to Nycho's famous Orca that was taken down from that same site because a giant billboard went up over it.

Hang a right at White Street and watch the street unfold with old school throw-ups for blocks.

MONTROSE STOP

Walk toward Meserole Street and after about a block you'll start seeing the leftovers of the Juicy Art Fest, where artists from all over the world gathered to paint up the industrial walls. The Sweat Shop's brick walls display some impressive work, from Pixel Pancho's (we love the guy) robotic half animals to Marka27's diabolic warrior to Dasic Fernandez' paint-melted half lady on the side of Fay Da Bakery's HQ.

Once you hit Waterbury Street, look left and cock your camera. The whole block is filled with murals on everything from walls to dumpsters. You'll see a fish with a NYC newsprint inlay, a few fishing Frenchmen (by Argentinian artist Ramiro Davaro-Comas), and Biggie watching precariously from the sidelines.

The coolest thing here is right in the middle of the block, where Jaz and Freddy Sam collaborate to create some Lucha Libre–looking characters (Jaz's signature) standing around a gazelle pyramid. Yeah, it's fucking weird and awesome. The end of the block has a cool piece by Palladino, which captures the spirit of Brooklyn perfectly via a trash-heavy surrealist face.

OTP Tip: A very well-known piece lingers nearby. Take a right on Scholes (the unmarked street at the end of the Waterbury art block) and walk up halfway. There, you'll see a mural by London's famed artist Stik, who leaves a little stick figure drawing wherever he goes. Also, Kremen's cool lioness is prowling right next to it.

JEFFERSON STOP

Start at Jefferson Street and Wyckoff Street

Much of the art you'll find here is curated by the Bushwick Collective, an organization started by Bushwick local Joe Ficalora, who saw a lot of love and loss in his neighborhood throughout the years. In an effort to beautify the place, Joe convinced business owners to allow artists to paint their walls. Now the hood is a lot more colorful, with international artists vying for spots to spray.

While you'll see snippets of things right off the subway stop, walk up Wyckoff Street to Troutman Street to get the whole shebang. Follow the BK boxing gloves onto Troutman, where you'll see all kinds of crazy shit. There's a flamingo on a fire hydrant done by Bronx legend James "Sexer" Rodriguez. A wacked-out Ninja Turtle sits in the middle of the block, drawn by cartoon-obsessed

Jerkface, whose murals of the Pink Panther, Mario Brothers, and the Cookie Monster decorate walls all over NYC.

The prized piece on Troutman is the deconstructed dog, done by Nychos, an artist all about blowing his paintings up into surreal anatomical cross-sections.

OTP Tip: Take a coffee break at AP Café (420 Troutman Street). It's the cleanest place in Bushwick.

The block wraps up with a requisite portrait of Biggie (this one by Danielle Mastrion), a water tower by Stik, and a black-and-white forest with ravens and bears by CJungle, a Russian duo.

When you hit Saint Nicholas Avenue, you'll see art on every corner. Proceed toward Pixel Pancho's robotic hand, swing a right on Cypress Avenue, then turn right on Starr Street, where another of his works, this time a reclining robot, is splayed out on a low wall.

At Starr and Saint Nicholas you'll see a mural of chickens painted on what looks like your typical industrial building. But this one is special. El Pollo Mas Bueno is some sort of mysterious livestock vendor and has live chickens (and rabbits, turkeys, pigeons, probably goats) walking around. You'll either be disgusted or super-hungry (in which case Tortillaria De Los Hermanos, with their fresh-off-the-press tacos, is a few steps away).

You've done a lot of walking and surely deserve a stiff drink ($6 shot and beer special, anyone?). Park it at Pearl's Social & Billy Club (40 Saint Nicholas Avenue), a ridiculous neighborhood bar where people go to get silly.

🏪 SHOP

MOLASSES BOOKS
#bookstore #cheap #coffee #beer
770 Hart Street

Got a dollar? Molasses has a whole rack of books you can buy. A comfy little used bookstore in Bushwick, this place is perfect when you want to get away from everything, spend a couple bucks on an interesting book, grab a coffee or beer (they sell both)—and read that bargain sucker on a bench by the window. The tunes here are all vinyl, and the shop holds poetry readings, book release parties, comedy shows, and other lit events pretty regularly.

SHOPS AT THE LOOM
#mini-mall #IndieDesigners #SmallBusinesses
1087 Flushing Avenue

The Loom is a cool collaboration of independent stores all operating in a mini-mall setting. This isn't your typical corporate-chain mall, but a collection of designers, yogis, and artisans, each contributing something to the space with their little store. Notably, the Loom is home to Gnostic Tattoo, Silky's screen printing and skate shop, Kávé espresso bar, Better Than Jam clothing and craft store, along with fifteen others. The Loom residents will often band together for events and community-building activities. Wandering through the hallways connecting the shops is like immersing yourself in a funhouse maze of shopping. Look for the secret green hallway exit.

URBAN JUNGLE
#ThriftStore #vintage
118 Knickerbocker Street

Urban Jungle fits the criteria for a legit, thrifty thrift shop blown up to massive proportions. Inside the huge warehouse space that's very well organized, items are grouped by type with seas of vintage jackets, rows of soft T-shirts, and more shoes than you can shake a foot at. Some of their items are downright weird, while others are quite wearable. The men's selection is huge, and this place rocks for purse whores, leather lovers, and those who love a good, productive dig. Prices are where they should be for secondhand, and creating a makeshift Halloween costume here works every time.

😊 PARTYING

ANCHORED INN
#bar #nautical
57 Waterbury Street

Washed up on an industrial concrete beach is the small but solid Anchored Inn. If bars could be tattoos, this one would be a buxom Sailor Jerry pinup. Covered in random portraits, dusty chandeliers, and seamen memorabilia (our personal fave is the creepy but oh-so-cool, early-twentieth-century diving outfit hanging from the ceiling), it'll make you think you're in Captain Hook's cabin. Draft microbrews are only $4 for happy hour, but the best deal is the $12 draft and burger special. There are outdoor benches when the weather's good that look out to some pretty iconic Brooklyn street art.

BIZARRE
#bar #sexy
12 Jefferson Street

Owned by two French dudes, this place is inherently sexier than your average American bar. For one, they've got absinthe . . . that they combine with tequila for a lethal cocktail that's a surefire panty-dropper. For deux, they put on burlesque shows with a whole lot of S&M-type action to keep things spicy. The drinks aren't cheap for the hood ($11–$12), but the place gets fun, rowdy, and supersexy.

BROOKLYN FIRE PROOF EAST
#bar #gallery #venue #party
119 Ingraham Street

Brooklyn Fire Proof is a complex that's comprised of sound stages (where all kinds of things are filmed and recorded), a shared workspace (for crafty Bushwickians to create their wares), and a public meeting place that's a café/bar/gallery and performance space. The café serves food made with things they grow in their own garden, there's a great patio, the gallery showcases some of the contemporary art coming out of the hood, and the performance space curates interesting music shows and thought-provoking performance art. Plus, they've got a $5 brunch and a twofer happy hour

BUSHWICK COUNTRY CLUB
#bar #dive #quirky
618 Grand Street

Put away the polos and boat shoes, this isn't that kind of country club. No, "Bushwick Country Club" is an ironic way of saying "shit-hole dive bar." Rumor has it that the owners are fans of *Caddyshack* and opened this bar in tribute. Love it or leave it, the Club is meant to be fun and dirty. Bar snacks are (free) Cheez Doodles, they've got board games and a booze slushie machine (Jim Beam slushies!), the bathroom is graffitied to shit, and you can (try to) play mini golf on the janky Astroturf in the backyard. Not quite a nice bar that has fallen into disarray, but more of an intentional dive, this bar is a good time if you're looking to down some PBRs and play a long, drunk game of Connect Four.

DUCKDUCK
#bar #karaoke
161 Montrose Avenue

Come here on Thursdays for their ear-busting karaoke and $5 vodka sodas. Their book of songs is expansive and has everything from the Stones to Lil Weezy. Duckduck attracts the perfect karaoke crowd, where most people are drunk enough to sing something funny and that one dude takes himself too seriously and does multiple songs in hopes of being discovered by a talent scout. Usually the karaoke gets the whole bar roaring, but if you'd like to hide out, there are couches on the right side to shield you from the off-key singing. The bathroom is a hilarious reminder that Brooklyn is tight on space.

GOODBYE BLUE MONDAY
#café #bar #venue #party
1087 Broadway Avenue

Ataxaphobics, beware: This place may make you shit your pants. Everyone else, say hello to one of your new favorite places on Earth—Goodbye Blue Monday. This coffee shop/bar/art gallery/music venue/antique thrift store/brunch spot has more shit going on than a normal person's brain can process in one visit. The anything-goes vibe is set with all the kitsch hanging from every square inch of wall and ceiling—it's like your aunt Millie's living room, if your aunt Millie were a Bushwick hipster and a borderline hoarder with better taste in art and music. With cheap beer ($2 PBRs, anyone?), burgers, and free shows almost every night, Goodbye Blue Monday is a welcome addition to any day of the week.

GOTHAM CITY LOUNGE
#bar #nerdy #GoodSpecials
1293 Myrtle Avenue

Appropriately named, Gotham is all about comic books. If you've got a secret stash of action figures you're too grown up to put out on the shelf, live vicariously through the décor at Gotham. Plastered on every wall and table, inside and out, you'll find comic books and collectibles that'll make your little geeky heart skip a beat. They've got insane drink specials, with $1 PBRs, or if you're channeling the Hulk, you can add a shot for only $2. It's dingy, small, and perfect.

OTP Tip: There's a Dominican food stall right outside that serves up $1 empanadas to make you feel like a superhero again until the morning.

PINEBOX ROCK SHOP
#bar #venue #vegan
12 Grattan Street

Pinebox Rock Shop is Bushwick's all-vegan, all-awesome bar and event venue. While you won't find clam juice in the Pinebox's Bloody Marys, you will find a whole lot of other shit you never knew could be stuffed into/onto a drink.

You'll get whatever pickled veggies they've got on hand (beets, onions, green beans, olives, etc.) on a skewer, along with a full-on celery stick. They also make their own Irish cream, so White Russians and Irish Car Bombs are still on the menu, and better than ever. The bathroom is a giant collage, the back room is all about karaoke, and they mix up their schedule of events to keep it fun every week, with a giant vegan market (Vegan Shop-Up) that takes over the space every other Saturday.

RADIO BUSHWICK
#LiveMusic #festivals
22 Wyckoff Avenue

Cuddled right next to the L train off Jefferson Street, Radio Bushwick is a music venue that hosts local music festivals and puts on indie shows. The kind of place you go to see your roommate's show for cheap. The space itself is pretty cool. From the outside, it's a wooden box with pinholes running down the sides; inside, the setup is intimate but blasts out great sound. They've also got a mod outdoor patio for chilling between sets.

RECLAMATION
#bar #GrandpaChic
817 Metropolitan Avenue

This hip, little, pretty place feels like a dreamy visit to the Prohibition Era. Rustic but simply gaudy, Reclamation Bar is "a new bar made from old things." Drink prices are standard, but the pours are generous and a semi-indoor smoking area makes the spot ideal if you hate being told to stand on the corner. With romantic lighting and large windows that fog when it's cold outside, it's a good place to bring a date but large enough to accommodate big groups too.

SILENT BARN
#LiveMusic #grungy
603 Bushwick Avenue

If you're looking for weird, Silent Barn is serving it up by the not-so-quiet ear- and eyeful. A collective of all kinds of artists, the space constantly changes to accommodate whatever weird performance rolls through. Silent Barn has a few artists in residence, which means that performances sometimes happen in its kitchen and living areas, complete with couches and a fridge. In addition to hosting underground bands and fun theme shows (dinosaur party, anyone?), you can also get a haircut at Deep Cuts and buy all kinds of crafty things from the small-shop owners who are part of the collective. Most shows are all ages.

TANDEM
#bar #GoodFood #DanceParty
236 Troutman Street

The kind of place where you let the day bleed into night, Tandem has a small but fantastic brunch menu, and lounging your way into happy hour, after which a dance party may erupt, is totally acceptable. To help you figure out what'll kill your midday hunger pangs, start off with their ridiculous Garden Bloody Mary. It's a pickled salad in a glass of bright red, beet-infused vodka that'll put your taste buds at attention. Proceed to the breakfast egg strata, a perfectly baked, pillowy dish that'll balance out the pickles and stomp out any remnants of last night's hangover. They have mozzarella pulled to order here, and if you've never had it outside of a plastic container, definitely find out what you've been missing by ordering it. While kale is on every menu from here to rural Iowa, Tandem does it up all lemony and tender, with white beans and Parmesan. When you're good and fed, stick around for happy hour, warm up your ankles, and wiggle your way to the room in the back, where dance parties pop off to reset your party circuits.

THE DRINK
#bar #nautical #BrokeFancy
228 Manhattan Avenue

This place is decorated with nautical rustic stuff the owners pulled from their basements and attics, and while they serve an assortment of drinks, go here for their spiked punch, concocted to fit the season and served in tiny teacups. The cold punch is great in the summer, when you can take full advantage of their all-white backyard. In the winter, their hot punch hits the spot. Now, these aren't your prom jungle-juice bowls of awful. These punches are meticu-lously crafted, with freshly extracted juices (like fucking pumpkin juice!), blended with chiles, teas, extracts, bitters, and syrups to create unique little prissy drinks that'll likely impress whoever you're trying to take to the captain's quarters.

THE GRAHAM
#bar #cheap
151 Meserole Street

The Graham offers nothing out of the ordinary, but we wouldn't want it any other way. Nothing-special décor, super-nice bartenders, cheap drinks, outdoor seating, free popcorn, and dollar tacos. A regular ol' bar for all of us regular people.

THE NARROWS
#bar #BrokeFancy #cocktails
1037 Flushing Avenue

An unexpected dose of classiness in the industrial, grimy part of Bushwick, the Narrows is where locals go when they've done their laundry and finally took a shower. The space is clean, prim, and proper, with a sleek bar decorated with simple shelves and manned by well-dressed bartenders. Their short menu of creative cocktails is decently priced (average $9 each), and the Babushka, a mix of vodka, ginger syrup, lime, and soda, is a refreshing, memorable concoction. This isn't the place you go to get shit-faced, but if you're feeling a little classier than usual, it's a good spot to hit for a taste of fancy mixology without the usual $14 price tag.

THE PAPER BOX
#venue #LiveMusic #party
17 Meadow Street

We don't know about you, but we've always had this ideal venue space in mind. Not the

most popular club in town where they make you stand outside like cattle. Not the small, musty indie space, which is cool sometimes when you don't mind having your rib cage elbow-reamed for a few hours. Not a huge space that never gets up to capacity and you can hear your straw hitting the bottom of the glass. The ideal space would be roomy, sparsely decorated, kind of in the middle of nowhere (for that danger element), with great acoustics and decent booze. Well, the Paper Box is that, hosting punk, electro-weirdness, and underground hip-hop shows, with two rooms and a backyard.

to harps. It's also connected to the Sweat Shop, Bushwick's prime rehearsal space where professionals and newly transplanted Midwesterners all gather to pull strings and beat up bass drums. The Wick is run by some New York music industry big shots who have managed clubs from Brooklyn to Ibiza. These dudes know what they're doing, and this space is a massive 8,000 square feet, with several levels and bars. The musicians they book vary across genres, and the "music fortress" accommodates music-hungry partiers well.

THE WICK
#LiveMusic #party
260 Meserole Street

Located in a multipurpose industrial building (which used to be a brewery), on any given weekend you'll see people coming in and out of the place with anything from guitars

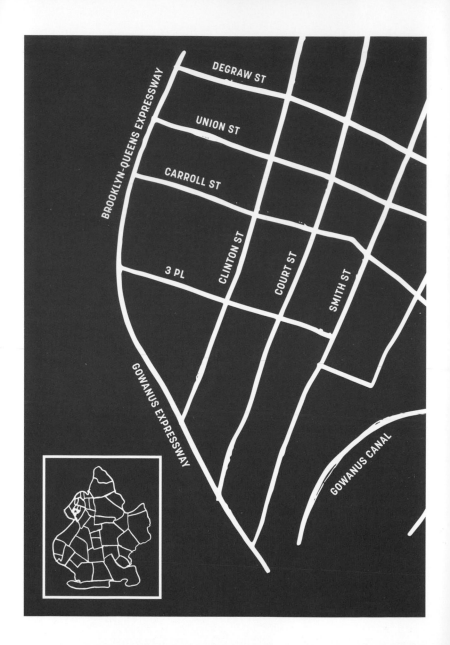

CARROLL

GARDENS

A little more grown up but still in the Brooklyn-know, Carroll Gardens is where you go to get a nice glass of wine, have a casual brunch, and watch the skater dads stroll about. You want a beautiful French pastry to pair with your morning coffee? Bien Cuit's got that. Some fancy prosciutto from real Italians? G. Esposito & Sons has been banging out the meaty stuff for generations. A bit of perfectly smoked fish from Shelsky's, a window-gazing walk down Court Street, and a well-crafted brew from 61 Local is how you do Carroll Gardens like a grown-up.

☕ COFFEE AND BAKERIES

BIEN CUIT
#croissants #bread
120 Smith Street

You might call yourself a croissant connoisseur, you may even be that douchebag who orders a pan au chocolate, but you've never really lived out your flaky pastry dreams until you've pulled apart the perfectly sweet, buttery, almond croissants artfully prepared at Bien Cuit. They bake them, slice them open to spread on a thick layer of nutty marzipan, and bake them again until they're perfectly bien cuit (or "well done"). While Bien Cuit can cover the costs of the operation on this incredible pastry alone, they actually have way more to offer. The chef is all about carbs (in the form of tarts and danishes), and they pump out the freshest, most beautiful bread you've ever seen, sold daily by the loaf or in sandwich form. Check out the bread sculptures around the yeasty-smelling shop, and if you decide to grab yourself a warm loaf, there are jams and spreads for sale in the back.

COURT PASTRY SHOP
#bakery #OldSchool #Italian
298 Court Street

A classic Italian bakery, they do cannolis like nobody else. Get a lobster tail on weekends. Fish? Oh, no, just a giant, croissant-like pastry, stuffed to the fins with pastry cream. They've got the cookies, tarts, and cakes that every nonna in the land knows how to make with her hands tied. None of this new-fangled shit that bakeries down the street make; Court Pastry sticks to the Italian classics and does them better than anybody else. The seating is nothing impressive, but you'll be so blinded by the sugary offerings that you won't care. Sit down with a cappuccino and an éclair to truly understand why this place has withstood the test of time.

KONDITORI
#coffee #pastries #juice #Swedish
114 Smith Street

Konditori is a mini-chain that blew up quick. In a sea of hyper coffee snobs who prefer their beans roasted in small batches from single origins, and competing with countrywide big-shots like Stumptown, Crop to Cup, and Intelligentsia, the Swedish beans in this place are in high demand. In addition to their unique coffee, Konditori bakes up some traditional Swedish pastries like kanelbulle, cardamom brod, and an array of coco balls and cookies (some of which are vegan). This location, of the several around the city, is not just a coffee shop but also shares the space with Farsk, a fresh juice bar. There's also a foosball table in the back for when you're so cracked-out that all you want to do is pull sticks to kick balls.

OTP Tip: The kid-to-adult ratio can sometimes get frighteningly close to 1:1.

VAN LEEUWEN ARTISAN ICE CREAM

#IceCream #artisan
81 Bergen Street

What started as a fancied-up ice-cream truck now has several brick-and-mortar locations around the city. Their approach to ice cream is unique in that instead of adding a bunch of shit to muddle your frozen cream into a sugar bomb of guilt, they pare it down to the basics, and improve upon it by focusing on the best possible ingredients to draw out maximum flavor. Their flavors, like vanilla, pistachio, and ginger, are clean and bold, with no need to add extras. Their philosophy translates into a streamlined shop, with just simple, botanical prints to illustrate the main ingredients in the flavors available. Every now and then, they'll make some more complicated concoction in small batches, but the owners stick to the classics to really get a feel for the ice cream that's made Van Leeuwen's a superstar in the business of sugar and cream.

EAT

BATTERSBY

#NewAmerican #TreatYourself
#TastingMenu
255 Smith Street

If you fancy yourself a foodie (and hate that word as much as we do), you will piss yourself at Battersby. The space is really small and romantic. As with most "foodie" restaurants, this place is a bit expensive. But their tasting menu (five- or seven-course) is substantial and, unlike a lot of places, will actually satisfy your hunger and not just your curiosity. Since Battersby's menus change seasonally, going during the spring, when ramps and new greens pop out of the ground, makes for the best experience. One thing that always remains on the menu is their house-made whipped ricotta that's drizzled with olive oil and served with a really good round of bread. That dish alone starts the meal at a very high point, and Battersby never drops the bar as the meal progresses. If you're really splurging, get the cocktail pairing.

FRANKIES 457

#ModernItalian #TreatYourself
#FreshPasta
457 Court Street

Frankies 457 is owned by two childhood friends, both named Frank, who grew up in Queens and reconnected after eighteen years of individual culinary exploration. Frankies was born from their combination of experiences with food and aims to pay homage to their shared Italian roots. On the fancy side of casual, Frankies serves seasonal Italian in an exposed-brick, airy setting with a nicely lit backyard. The food here is crafted with intention, their pasta is made in-house, and the cheeses are carefully sourced. The house-made ricotta is super-fluffy, their prosciutto is like salty candy, and all of their crostinis are balanced bites. Get anything with sausage or meatballs in it, then follow up with a bowl of perfectly al dente linguine (the $20 squid-ink dish, if you really stopped giving a fuck about your budget). The Franks top it all off with a reasonably-priced, expertly paired selection of wines.

G. ESPOSITO & SONS

#meat #Italian #MonsterSandwiches
257 Court Street

Walking into G. Esposito & Sons will feel like you're part of a big Italian family. The staff is comprised of guys who'll call you "boss" and make you feel like they've known you since elementary school. If the hanging meat doesn't tip you off, this shop is all about making their goods the old-fashioned way, and you'll find a huge variety of salumi. While they used to be exclusively a pork shop (all of their piggy products are top-notch by the way), they're now a full-service meat store, with incredible sandwiches and rice balls. G. Esposito & Sons doesn't fuck around with dainty sandwiches either; each of their between-bread creations is stuffed full of thinly sliced meats and cheeses. The meatball sub alone is enough for a day's worth of good eating (if you could only make it last). Don't let the terrifying pig statue outside deter you from experiencing the warm and welcoming vibes and eats inside.

LUCALI
#pizza #TreatYourself
575 Henry Street

To keep his childhood candy store from being turned into a corporate crap business, Mark Lacono bought this space and created Lucali. If you want to get really close and personal with your pizza, Lucali has an open kitchen where you can watch the chefs stretch, fill, and fire up your pizza. A small space, the whole joint smells like smoke, and when you finally get your pizza, eating it is a whole-face experience. The thin crust bubbles up in their wood-fired oven, and the stringy, melty cheese is charred just right. Great for pizza purists, as Lucali only serves pizzas and calzones with limited toppings. They do these things well, and the dining experience, while kind of pricey, will be something you'll remember with all your senses.

SHELSKY'S OF BROOKLYN
#bagels #lox
141 Court Street

Mastering and redefining the art of "appetizing," this shop is a tribute to the immigrant-fueled bagel-and-lox scene of the OG LES. While Shelsky's sells a lot of little things that may interest you, their fish is the superstar. Shelsky's has the cold-smoked classics, like gravalax and nova, and some tasty new world additions, like spicy Mexican achiote and our favorite, the pastrami lox. Throw some on a bagel with schmear or, if you want to fancy up the experience, get the Bentowitz box, a jewified bento box that you can fill with side salads (make sure a half-sour pickle is in the mix), fish, and bread for a full meal.

So you managed to get yourself a date, you sly cat! Now there's the daunting task of impressing a stranger in an unfamiliar city. We got your back. Here are a few spots that'll make you look like you got this romance thing down.

ALMA ROOFTOP

Alma (187 Columbia Street) sits like a big boner on the Columbia waterfront. It's three stories high, with a bar on the first level and the restaurant dining rooms occupying the second and rooftop levels. Up at the top, the panoramic view of the Manhattan skyline is unparalleled.

IKEA BEDROOM DISPLAY

So you spent all your pizza money on booze. Luckily, romance can still be found for nothing at all. Taking your date to IKEA is a scary step in the domestic direction, but this particular particleboard dealer comes with a sexy view. Wiggle up to the showroom, sit on a few couches, play house in their nonfunctional kitchens, and avoid making impulse purchases. The bedroom displays are the cheap date hot spot. Facing the Red Hook waterfront, hop on a MALM and watch the sunset, then have a few meatballs to seal the Swedish deal.

ROOTS N' RUCKUS

Every Wednesday at 9:00 p.m., the Jalopy School of Music (315 Columbia Street) throws down an eclectic (and free) folk show led by a musical maniac named Feral Foster. The old-timey space, lined with church pews and theater props, showcases amazing fiddle players and throaty singers. Wine is served in mason jars at the café up front, and the adjacent bar absorbs the postshow overflow, where private encores and impromptu performances always break out.

JAKEWALK

The setup at Jakewalk (282 Smith Street) is perfect for two. Their $16 fondue for two comes with green apples, salami, and bread. The room is dimly lit, they have excellent wine, and dipping things into cheese then pulling them out is pure mouth sex. "Jake Walk" refers to the stiff leg affliction people would get drinking jungle-juice booze during Prohibition. Luckily, all the alcohol here isn't permanently debilitating, but you may still end up with a stiffy if you play your cards right.

THE CHOCOLATE ROOM

Put your date on the fast track to diabetes because the Chocolate Room (269 Court Street) is basically made of cocoa. You'll walk in and be hit with a display case stuffed with truffles and a cake stand holding the tallest, brownest chocolate cake you've ever seen. Get a seat in the back near the wall-to-ceiling windows that overlook the fairytale backyard. Pick your poison (cake, it's always cake), get a few glasses of wine, and blissfully slip into a sugar coma.

 SEE AND DO

THE INVISIBLE DOG ART CENTER
#gallery #multimedia
51 Bergen Street

Every time we walk by this place, someone is setting up a show that looks amazing. The shows here are always pensive, with a sense of humor. Dealing with topics like death, war, and human angst, the ideas at Invisible Dog are represented in all mediums from visual art to performance and film. They encourage their artists to collabo, and some amazing, multimedia stuff comes out of the process. Come here to think, drink, and laugh.

CARROLL GARDENS GREENMARKET
#tiny #FreeSamples
Carroll and Smith Streets

Every Sunday from 8 a.m. until 4 p.m., local vendors and farmers bring the best of what they've grown down to Carroll street. This market is tiny and filled with stroller-pushing moms, but on a nice day it'll feel like a small town in the middle of the country. Sample little turkey meatballs from Dipola Turkey to get your appetite rolling for lunch and pick up an artisan loaf from Bread Alone. The produce is always top-notch and the market is open year-round.

SHOP

BUFFALO EXCHANGE
#ThriftShop #NewVintage
109 Boerum Place

This Buffalo Exchange is the newer location of the two in Brooklyn. It sells very recent fashions with some vintage pieces you'll have to dig for to find. This store is clean, well organized, and split fairly evenly into men's and women's sections. For the ladies, you'll find a lot of dresses that reflect what the women in the neighborhood are sporting. Since there are a lot of young moms, their pre-preggo wear is now available for your browsing pleasure. The gents have several racks of denim, T-shirts, and nice jackets to pick through. The shoe and accessory collection at this location is fantastic as well.

CAPUTO'S FINE FOODS
#HomemadeRicotta #Italian
#SpecialtyFood
460 Court Street

Come in, take a number. When your turn comes up, go straight for the jugular and get the mozzarella. Pulled in-house, it's the smoothest, freshest-tasting white blob you'll ever try. An Italian specialty foods store, Caputo's also makes their own fresh pastas, ricotta, sauces, and olives and sells a nice variety of imported cheeses. The cannolis here are the real deal and filled with ricotta to order. If you're looking to go beyond the pasta box, Caputo's will hook you up with the things you need (lobster ravioli!) to create an Italian family meal your hostelmates or couchsurfing host will never forget.

HOMAGE
#SkateShop #sneakers
460 Court Street

A shop filled with the brand's boards and all
kinds of kicks, come here to shop for decks
covered in art and all the accessories you
need to roll down the street in style. The
staff is friendly and not skate-snobby, so
they'll hook you up with just the right stuff.
They hold workshops and are up on the culture enough to direct you to a good park to
test out your buys. They've got a mini-ramp
inside and sometimes hold events that allow
you to jump that ramp. If you're itching to
ride right away, there are some skateable
cement blocks on the way back to the train.

STINKY BKLYN
#cheese #meats
215 Smith Street

If your nose craves something beyond Kraft
Singles, it'll be smacked silly when you walk
into Stinky. First decide how deep you want
to get into the smelly cheese cave, then sample a few of their divinely stinky cheeses. We
like ours extra rotten, so we tend to go for
whatever ashy, oozing, blue variety they've
got in the shop. You want meat with that?
Stinky carves up all kinds of cured meats, like
wild boar salami and Spanish *jamón serrano*.
To complement the salt and funk, they also
sell locally made sweets and condiments.
And beer, tons of beer, some on tap. You can
marry all the goods in the form of a sandwich
or get anything you want by weight. Gotta
have that funk!

PARTYING

61 LOCAL

#bar #coffee #CraftBeer
61 Bergen Street

When you start to outgrow kegs and shots, 61 Local is there to pick up the aging pieces. A grown-up beer bar (and café during the day), this place is a nice, open, all-wood space that serves mostly local craft beers. While it's laid out like a beer garden, nothing ever gets too rowdy here. A great spot to get an afternoon (or early-evening) beer and discuss who's banging who, but at a more adult volume. If you're not completely exhausted on mustaches, you'll find an etched one on the bathroom mirror. Be warned that Carroll Gardens is full of strollers, and miserable drunk moms will bring their kids into this place, which sometimes creates a toddler obstacle course.

CAMP

#bar #smores
179 Smith Street

Perhaps it's the mounted kayak, or the camp lounge seating in the back, but this place brings us right back to our camp-going childhoods. The bar conversations we've overheard here usually involve drinking games and ghost stories. There's Big Buck Hunter, a fireplace, a Dirty Girl Scout cocktail, and other campy things. We don't know about you, but our favorite part of camp (aside from the naughty counselors), was making our own s'mores, and this place will bring those warm campfire feelings right back. You can order DIY s'mores, which consist of wrapped Hershey's bars, a package of graham crackers, a pile of marshmallows, and a little pot of fire so you can get toasty and tipsy all at once.

GOWANUS YACHT CLUB

#bar #dive #quirky
323 Smith Street

Everyone knows that yachts wouldn't survive a day on the filthy Gowanus, and this fake social club is too silly to be taken seriously. A shack that opens up every summer right above the Carroll Street F/G stop, the Yacht Club is an outdoor beer dive. Wooden stakes greet you at the shabby entrance, and you'll discover after walking inside that the whole thing is nothing more than a makeshift beer counter and a few picnic benches. You can get typical bar food ($5 burgers, $2-$6 dogs) with your beers (except they don't do fries) and spend the day hanging out with very unambitious drunkards. They open midday and close whenever the fuck they feel like it.

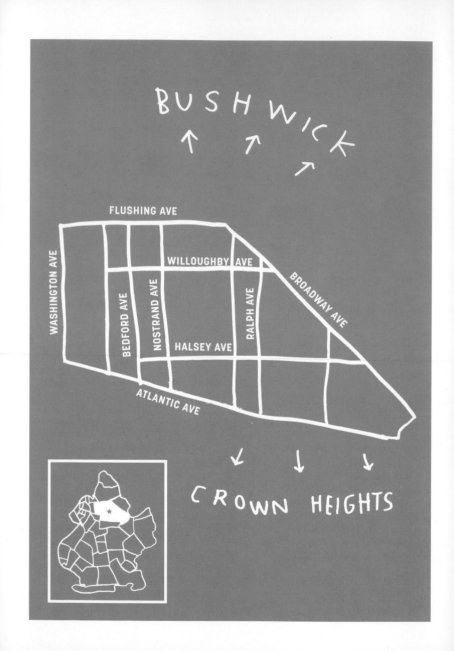

CLINTON HILL/
BED-STUY

While these are technically two different neighborhoods, the perceived borders keep changing as gentrification expands. But no matter where the lines are drawn, Bed-Stuy will always be about Biggie, Crown Fried Chicken, and unscrewed fire hydrants in the summertime. The hood where hip-hop got its cool, Bed-Stuy may be a little less "do or die" these days but walking around will still get you in the thick of things. The residents here are very diverse, the streets are speckled with characters, and on any given day, somebody is blasting old-school jams from their car stereo. Home to the Pratt Institute, go here to see what inspired Jay Z, Mos Def, Spike Lee, and many other creative legends, and pet a few bodega cats while you're at it.

COFFEE AND BAKERIES

BROOKLYN KOLACHE CO.

#coffee #kolaches #CoolDécor
520 DeKalb Avenue

This coffee shop brings the forgotten (or never heard of ever) kolache to the Brooklyn baked-goods playing field. A kolache is a little round of dough that cradles either savory or sweet fillings in the middle. It originated in Eastern Europe and found major popularity in Texas. This shop fills their Texan treats with stuffings like jalapeño, cheddar, eggs, sausage, apricot, strawberry, and sweet cheese. Kolaches aside, the space is designed very well. There are two rooms and a spacious, tree-and-bench backyard that gets great sun in the summer. The whole thing has a very industrial but somehow comfortable vibe with mason jars, reclaimed items, tin accents, and interesting metallic art. The kolaches are all made in-house in the bakery space right in the middle of the shop, and they hold movie nights (with an old-school popcorn machine!) and parties in the back room.

CLEMENTINE BAKERY

#bakery #cakes #vegan
299 Greene Avenue

While they don't advertise themselves as such, everything here is vegan. A tiny little neighborhood bakery, Clementine feels like you've stepped into a breezy café off some dreamy European cobblestone street. Clementine is a cool sort of cute that's less princess birthday party and more cup of tea at high noon. The display cases have tall, creamy cakes, sweet and savory scones and biscuits, muffins, danishes, bars, and plump cinnamon rolls (if you catch them on a weekend). The coffee isn't great, but the girls bake up a storm in the kitchen right behind the counter, and everyone is high on vegan compassion, so the service is always stellar. During the summer, they do ice cream, and getting a slice of their luscious chocolate cake, with a scoop of vanilla, is an awesome way to spend an afternoon.

DOUGH

#doughnuts #bakery #FamousFood
305 Franklin Avenue

There's been quite a bit of hype about gourmet doughnuts sweeping New York in the past few years, and Dough has been pivotal to the revolution. While the Donut Plant maintains a stronghold on Manhattan, Dough continues to take the cake as Brooklyn's best. Served up at the Williamsburg Smorgasburg, at a spattering of Brooklyn

Urban Vintage

coffee shops, and at their original Bed-Stuy storefront, these fluffy yet dense, oh-so-delicately glazed concoctions are the most fabulous doughnuts we've ever had. Creative toppings make them as unique as Brooklyn—the dulce de leche is a must try, as is the perfectly tart sweet hibiscus

OUTPOST

#coffee #backyard #GoodMusic
1014 Fulton Street

Outpost is the ideal Brooklyn café. Eclectic, repurposed furnishings? Check. Ironic photographs and art pieces? Done. Good coffee, the right kind of small bites, wine at night, a playlist that'll negate your need to plug your ears up with headphones? All there. Most of the baristas aren't sugary nice but have that thrift-store fashionista thing on lock. While some strollers do make their way out to this part of town, most of the regulars are young locals looking to get their fix. Outpost outdoes your average café with their expansive, fairyland backyard. Way more than a dinky strip of concrete, the

yard at Outpost is a trilevel wonderland of seating, potted plants, lights, and canopies. There's even a plug out there, should you want to do a little work in the fresh air.

URBAN VINTAGE

#coffee #sweets #jewelry #CoolDécor
204 Grand Street

Urban Vintage is a large space that sprawls across half of the block. Some of the baristas can be gritty, and despite its expansiveness, a seat is often hard to come by. If you make it past these obstacles, you will be rewarded with great coffee and a nice view. The décor is velvety vintage, with bistro tables, mismatched chairs, couches, and long curtains tied off to expose the all-window walls that wrap around the place. Everything here is reasonably priced, including the cheaper-than-most cup of coffee, plus they have macaroons and cakes to fancy the whole thing up. When you're waiting for your drink, take a look at the handmade jewelry, crafts, and other wares displayed on the thrifty cabinets.

 # EAT

CHOICE MARKET
#lunch #French #PicnicPerfect
#BakedGoods
318 Lafayette Avenue

A small space with one communal table and ample outdoor seating, Choice is a coffee shop/eatery specializing in prepared foods. Sounds simple enough, but wow is it complex. They don't just pump out stale salads and sandwiches. At Choice, things are French fancy. Their available items change frequently, but on any given day there'll be some sort of juicy, slow-cooked meat, creative pasta dishes, healthy salads, and swirly-whirly baked goods galore. The place is super-popular, and the line fills up the whole store, all day, every day. The trick here is to eye-shop from line and make your decisions quick as you move along. Everything is sold by weight, and while you may end up with more than you can swallow, you'll be surprised at how hard it'll be to stop eating.

CROWN FRIED CHICKEN
#HoodChicken #JayZ
822 Myrtle Avenue

A popular hood chicken joint, Crown's bird is super-crispy on the outside, juicy on the inside, and comes in red box buckets like it should. It'll be a little greasy but perfect for a late-night binge (the popcorn chicken combo will hit the munchies spot). The atmosphere is that of a small fast-food joint, but this particular location has some furniture that others don't. Namely, a picture of Jay Z . . . because he used to work there.

DO OR DINE
#TreatYourself #WackyAsFuck
#FoodNetwork #FoieGrasDoughnut
1108 Bedford Avenue

If the name doesn't tip you off, this place is pretty wacky. You know when you were a kid and decided to get all Iron Chef on whatever was in the fridge after school? Well this place, headed by *Food Network Star* winner Justin Warner, is a successful version of that. The out-of-the-box creations here will make you forget all about the ketchup-glazed TV dinners with leftover tuna casserole crumble disasters of your youth. Justin takes things like duck and pairs it with kiwi; his fish and chips is an actual, whole deep-fried fish; and he makes "crab cakes" out of jellyfish. Everything here has a certain creative sense of humor, and he hits it out of the imaginative park with the, now famous, foie gras doughnut. This isn't just adventurous eating; getting a table here means relinquishing your right to wince at weirdness.

KENNEDY FRIED CHICKEN

#HoodChicken #DrunkFood
357 Nostrand Avenue

This will be the greasiest chicken you've ever had the displeasure to put near your face. The service will be slow and inattentive. The atmosphere is really just walls, a counter, and maybe a chicken bone or two in a far corner. You will wonder how Kennedy's keeps its door open among the endless selection of much better food options. They've been around since before Bed-Stuy was "up and coming." Many people eat here for nostalgic reasons; you should probably only eat here if you're drunk enough to not care. Undoubtedly worse than KFC, Kennedy is hood chicken and makes regular appearances in rap songs.

PEACHES HOTHOUSE

#Southern #SpicyFriedChicken
415 Tompkins Avenue

If you're craving something spicy with a comforting Southern kick, Peaches Hothouse hooks you up with the crunchiest, double-spiciest chicken on this side of the Mason-Dixon line. A Nashville-style joint, they've got all the classic favorites like catfish (in nugget and blackened form), grits, collard greens, and delicious smoked meats. But come here for their hot chicken ($13) that pairs perfectly with the juicy, cooling watermelon salad. The ambiance isn't something to really speak about, but you shouldn't talk with all that hot bird in your mouth anyway.

PILAR CUBAN EATERY

#lunch #ModernCuban
397 Greene Avenue

Cuban food, with its sloppy beans and greasy plantains, tends to be a messy experience. While Pilar still hawks at-least-three-napkin food, it's a bit more refined. All that aggressive flavor is still there, but the portions are manageable and you don't feel gypped because everything here is stewed down until all of the flavors meld into a paradisiacal mouthful. If all you've ever had of Cuban food is the classic Cuban sandwich, Pilar's authentic version won't disappoint. To go beyond the common, get yourself a plate of pernil, or citrusy mojo-marinated pork so juicy and tender your teeth'll feel left out. It comes with "RBP," or "rice, beans, and sweet plantains," which all complement the pork by adding sweetness and texture. Pilar's menu items are on a weekly rotation, with brunch items available on Sunday.

SARAGHINA

#FancyPizza #HomestyleVibe #romantic
435 Halsey Street

Bed-Stuy isn't all BBQ and Chinese, and this little gem transports diners to a happier time before anyone ever needed to Do the Right Thing. Skip the lines at Roberta's and hit up this place instead, where chefs cook the way their mothers did—with love and good ingredients. You won't find groundbreaking recipes, but the quaint, country-cottage décor feels pretty damn groundbreaking in this hood. It's considerably cheaper, too, than its gourmet pizza counterparts in other neighborhoods, and the salads alone are worth taking a longer train ride.

SCRATCH BREAD

#bakery #5BuckBrunch #BadassBread
1069 Bedford Avenue

Something about this place is sort of punk. Sure, baking is a precise science that should have nothing to do with sloppy punk, but the fact that they don't hold back on the black

pepper and create jagged pastries that aren't quite prim and proper, gives them that same assertive edge. Hawking their goods from a window in Bed-Stuy, Scratch Bread is a ballsy bakery and innovative breakfast/lunch maker. They serve all kinds of things, like grits and the thickest cut, perfectly rendered bacon you can imagine. They know that their breads pair best with gooey, soft-boiled eggs that permeate the chewy bits, and they'll put an egg on just about anything. They have a "breadule" or schedule of which breads are available when. You can build your own pizza and grits, and their packed-with-flavor sauces (like the almond romanesco and Italian-gone-Mex Sicilian salsa verde) are available by the half pint. For something sweeter, the chai pecan sticky buns will pull out your molars, leaving you joyfully toothless.

SPEEDY ROMEO

#pizza #CreativeDishes
376 Classon Avenue

Run by two friends, Speedy Romeo captures the essence of what these guys care about in life: food and fun. The food here is pizza, the fun comes from the toppings on these pizzas and ordering them by name. The White Album, a nod to the Beatles, is the perfect white pizza with a creamy béchamel, a mix of melted cheeses, and crispy crust. The Dan-

gerfield (Rodney) is definitely a heart attack on a plate, with meatballs and an oozy egg baked into the toppings. Their Saint Louie is a ballsy move as it opens up the Midwesterner criticism flood gates. Luckily, everyone agrees that they do this distinctive style of pizza justice by not holding back on processed Provel and cutting it in squares the way those crazy Missourians like it. Aside from great pizza, they start you off with pickled hot peppers, and, if you need a bit more, the stuffed pepper appetizer is great. The atmosphere is nice and dark, so you won't feel bad when you shove chocolate cake with marshmallows and graham crackers (their take on s'mores) down the gullet to finish off the meal.

◉ SEE AND DO

PRATT INSTITUTE

#ArtSchool #SculptureGarden
#EngineRoomRelic
200 Willoughby Avenue

The outdoor spaces of Brooklyn's big-deal art school are fun to explore. There are random sculptures along the walkways; some are cool, others look like a poor attempt at pottery. Our favorite thing to do on campus is wander around the engine room, a strange relic from the turn of the century right in the middle of the school, which not only houses a big old engine but also a bunch of dirty, unfriendly cats. You can walk right in if the door is open and read all about the room, while listening to the crazy sounds inside.

BED-STUY

Listen close to the east coast rap of the '90s and you'll hear lyrics dedicated to Bed-Stuy, a neighborhood where few dared to go but where many got their start. The Junior M.A.F.I.A. was a group of kids who hung out together on the stoops and streets; everyone had regular jobs in the hood (with some drug dealing on the side), and these then-rough streets inspired some of the most recognizable beats and words of the recent past. Bed-Stuy has transformed since those days, with less crack and more organic kale, and arguably less soul. But these historic hip-hop spots still stand, albeit among different surroundings. Pop on some old-school jams by Biggie, Lil' Kim, and Black Star to soundtrack your journey into hip-hop's past.

BAG IT WITH BIGGIE

The Met supermarket on Fulton Street (between Cambridge Place and Saint James Place) isn't notorious for its groceries. In addition to dealing drugs on local corners,

Biggie held down a legit job as a bag boy here. Maybe pick up some sardines for dinner, then hang around on the corner of Saint James and Fulton to feel transported to the "Juicy" video. Re-create his walk home by heading to 226 Saint James Place, loitering on the stoop for a while, and trying to get people to call you Big Poppa.

Bonus: If you've really got some mad skills, pick a battle on the corner of Bedford Avenue and Quincy Street, where Biggie whooped some major lyrical ass back in 1991. Do a pull-up off the traffic light for good measure.

OL' DIRTY BASTARD MURAL

After his OD death in 2004, a mural of Dirty's welfare card, with his signature and everything, was blown up and painted in his honor at 126 Putnam Avenue. The mural has been written on repeatedly for the last ten years, with some people throwing up praises to ODB and Wu-Tang, and a few haters in the mix. Ironically, there's an ATM in the bodega on which the mural's painted. So, baby, you can get money, don't you worry.

LIL' KIM

Biggie's bestie Kim has been around the Bed-Stuy block, and the video to one of her first singles was a tribute to her hood. Stand on the corner of Dean Street and Nostrand Avenue, on location of the video, and don't forget to put your lighter(s) up. Decking yourself out in all Brooklyn-logo gear and chains is totally optional (please don't).

JAY Z'S STOOP

It has been said that Jay Z spent his formative years sitting on a stoop, bobbing his head like he does to the beats that blared in his headphones, schizo-spitting lyrics as they came to him. Head over to the Marcy Projects (452 Marcy Avenue) and find a place to perch for a while. If nothing Roc-A-Fella-worthy comes to you, get the fuck out—it's still the projects after all.

For a taste of the chicken that paid Jigga's bills, hit up Crown Fried Chicken (822 Myrtle Avenue) where the man himself worked.

NO MORE MOS

A few years ago, if you hung around Nostrand Avenue long enough, you'd see Mos Def walking around doing regular things. Since he moved to Cape Town, South Africa, recently, and started asking that we call him by his real name, Yasiin Bey, you won't find him lingering around the hood much. If you want to get super stalky, head to the Roosevelt Houses (153 DeKalb Avenue) where Mos grew up after moving from Jigga's neck of the woods.

TALIB KWELI

Mos Def's complementary other half of Black Star used to live a block off Myrtle Avenue. Back then, though, it was called "Murder Avenue." Take a stroll around now and you'd have to try mighty hard to get close to murdered with all the fancy restaurants and poppin' bars.

SHOP

CLINTON HILL PICKLES
#pickles
431 DeKalb Avenue

A rebranded version of a popular, now defunct LES shop (Guss' Pickles), you will come here for a cucumber pickle and leave with all kinds of vegetables and fruit you've never dreamed of pickling. They've got pickled beets, cauliflower, mango, peppers, olives, tomatoes, mushrooms, kraut, and other salty-sour things floating in huge barrels. Plus, you get to choose how "pickly" your cucumbers are. From lightly-brined new pickles to face-scrunching full sours, the pickles here are perfect for using as vodka chasers, piling on sandwiches, or just munching straight up like a pickle fiend.

MISS MASTER'S CLOSET
#ThriftStore #Designer

On a lonely stretch of Bedford Avenue, Miss Master's is a thrifting gem. While it may look like an expensive boutique, decorated with antique couches and triple-paneled mirrors, most things here are reasonably priced. The selection is small but well curated, with beautiful vintage dresses lining the walls and color-coded racks of incredible finds for both sexes. Once you've picked through your fill of vintage, head to the counter where you'll find stylish sunglasses (and those pretend reading glasses) for $5.

PARTYING

BLACK SWAN

#bar #BeerDoneRight #classy
#LocalFavorite
1048 Bedford Avenue

One of the first swank spots to open in Bed-Stuy (right next door to a KFC), Black Swan doesn't look like much. But once you part its huge doors, you'll enter a long, expansive hall to a place that serves beer in their appropriately shaped glasses and along with extraordinary gastropub eats. Black Swan hosts game nights, which are usually packed but less meatheady than other sports bars. They also serve an amazing brunch (rum French toast, in case you need guidance) with a full bar drink menu. Black Swan is the kind of place you go on Friday night to schmooze the shit out of all the locals, then return midday Saturday and share hangover stories with those same, slightly more puffy faces.

DYNACO

#bar #cozy #fireplace
1112 Bedford Avenue

While most bars smell like vomit, Dynaco smells of burning wood because this homey joint has a wood-burning fireplace that's perfect for when NYC shits snow all over your plans. The wooden interior is cozy, and the repurposed speakers make for nice divider walls. The drinks here are well made, and the bartenders will listen to your weather complaints all night over some whiskey and a piece of cake. You'll want to cuddle, which will morph into making out.

TIP TOP BAR & GRILL

#bar #dive #DrunkDancing
432 Franklin Avenue

Nothing is ironic or worn-down on purpose; everything is legitimately grimy and fabulous. The tunes are stuck on '90s hip-hop, the beers are $5, and the bathroom will make you feel like a filthy skank. It takes years of beating a place to shit for it to get into such a state, and Tip Top has aged perfectly. While it may look like an anything-goes establishment, they have a sign that says "absolutely no drugs, you are being watched." Do your drugs elsewhere; do your drunk dancing here.

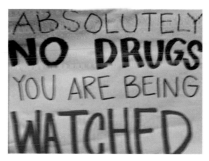

FLASH BACK

FULTON MALL

The Fulton Street Mall is an outdoor corridor in Downtown Brooklyn, with a rich history that currently sits as the embodiment of the hard-to-define idea of gentrification. People are careful with their words when it comes to talking about the topic because at its core, gentrification forces Americans to pick apart their lingering racism, from all sides.

The Fulton Street Mall used to be a creative mecca for surrounding residents, where people would buy the wares that came to define the style of '80s and '90s Brooklyn. Sneakers, gaudy gold chains, hats, and other swag were sold for rock-bottom prices, and the mall was a place where some of hip-hop's greatest hung out, got their hair did, and

picked up honeys. All that stuff we nostalgic hip-hop heads remember came from Fulton Street Mall.

Fulton Street Mall was also crime-ridden back then; or at least those who didn't "belong" there thought so. We're not going to argue that crack and drive-bys weren't rampant, but the Fulton Street Mall had more to it than that.

Since the 2004 "cleanup," the mall has transformed. As the crime rate dropped, the mall began to bleed out culture. Macy's and Starbucks came down with the corporate hammer, forcing long-standing businesses to close shop, and profits were redirected into the pockets of people not interested in preserving this cultural landmark. Tense conversations arose and civil rights–era phrases like "white businesses" resurfaced in the debate.

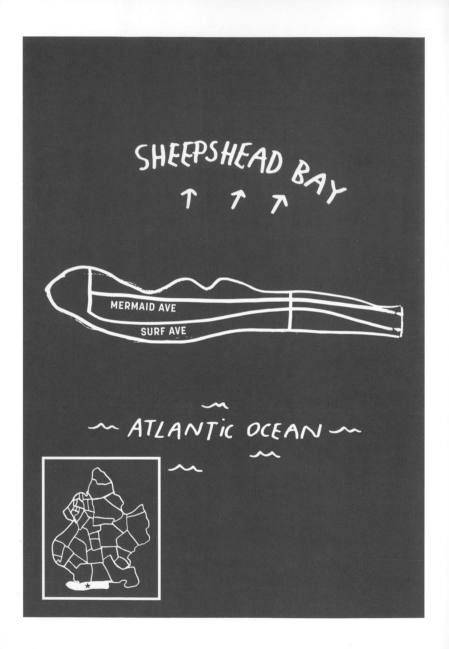

CONEY ISLAND

The terminal stop on the F, N, D, and Q trains lands you right in the midst of this country's iconic, freak-show landmark. While Coney Island has been somewhat pillaged by larger corporations looking to set up shop, some of the historical businesses have survived the "renovation." The boardwalk along the beach offers you a glimpse into the older, more circus-like side of Brooklyn. During the warmer months, people still put on acts in full carney fashion, and while many places are a little hokey, when the Mermaid Parade rolls through every summer, you're guaranteed an eyeful of weird. Although Sandy beat the amusement out of the park in 2012, most of it has been pieced back together and refreshed. With the iconic Deno's Wonder Wheel, whiplash-inducing Cyclone, fluffy wads of cotton candy, sideshows, and Nathan's Famous Hot Dog Eating Competition, hitting Coney Island is essential even if the only thing you do there is ask Zoltar for advice.

COFFEE AND BAKERIES

RITA'S ITALIAN ICE

#FrozenCustard #ItalianIce

1327 Surf Ave

Escaping the summer heat is made easier at Rita's, located right across from the boardwalk. To cool your mouth, Rita's serves frozen desserts of the old-school variety. Go for the gelati, a best-of-both worlds layering of Italian ice on the bottom with a swirl of creamy custard on top. Go ahead and throw a few toppings over it like nobody's watching and take it for a stroll on the boardwalk.

🍔 **EAT**

NATHAN'S FAMOUS
#HotDogs #FamousFood
1310 Surf Avenue

There are better hot dogs around; there, we said it. But Nathan's is one of those iconic places that needs to happen if you find yourself in BK. Right on the boardwalk, their signature hot dogs are best enjoyed as part of the full Coney Island experience, complete with sideshow freaks and roller coaster riding. Most Brooklyn natives grew up on Nathan's and make a trip out every now and then to hit their nostalgia buttons. You (and a million other tourists) can have the experience, regardless of where you were raised. They've got a bunch of other things on the menu (like burgers, cheesesteaks, and such), but don't kid yourself; grab a dog and fries, and suck them down on the large patio. If you're looking to eat the dogs and avoid the lines, go there in the winter when the annual contest is at least six months away. If you're a fan of getting your elbows in mustard and sauerkraut on your crotch, go there on the Fourth of July at 10:00 a.m.

TOTONNO'S
#OldSchool #pizza #FamousFood
1524 Neptune Avenue

Food here isn't artisanal in any way, it's just downright damn good pizza. The ingredients are fresh, used in the right proportions, and expertly baked. It's the kind of pizza shop that'll spark nostalgia rather than offer a refined dining experience. Close to the Coney Island boardwalk, Totonno's makes their pies in a coal oven, with superthin crusts and a tangy, slightly sweet sauce. They capture the essence of old-world NYC pizza in every way, as evidenced by their décor, which is just a cluttered wall of "celebrity" photos.

FUN FACT

Catch-22 writer, Joseph Heller, was born in Coney Island in 1923 and spent his childhood running around the boardwalk.

SEE AND DO

CONEY ISLAND MUSEUM
#Americana #oddities
1208 Surf Avenue

Dedicated to preserving the iconic pop culture of Coney Island, this museum is filled with all kinds of memorabilia from the glory days of Coney. Open approximately between Easter and Halloween, the museum is full of sideshow stuff, like out-of-use ride parts, a good bit of oddball taxidermy, carney posters, and painted signs that date back as far as 1829. They also hold classes, workshops, and have artists in residence to promote the creation of art related to that crazy scene. The museum hosts seaside sideshows, burlesque shows, and a variety of spectacles to keep the carney spirit alive.

LUNA PARK
#rides #games
1000 Surf Avenue

Coney Island is "America's Beach," and Luna Park is where the rides live. Though this seaside amusement park recently got an update, the classic rides, mixed in with new

thrills, are still around to take you back to a childhood you wish you had. A $32 wristband gets you four hours of unlimited amusement, or you can purchase credits ($1 each or bulk deals) and pay per coaster, which ranges from three (kiddie rides) to twenty (Slingshot) credits each. You can't leave without riding the Cyclone (not included in the unlimited wristband deal), an iconic wooden roller coaster built in 1927—the second oldest in the world—which will likely dislocate a few vertebrae while making you laugh-cry.

OTP Tip: Deno's Wonder Wheel is also excluded from the wristband deal. To experience one of the only Ferris wheels with moveable cars, you'll need to pony up $7.

THE MERMAID PARADE
#SeaFreaks #Floats
starts at W. 21st Street and Surf Avenue

Like a summer Halloween but fishier, the Mermaid Parade has rolled through Coney Island for thirty years with the mission of inspiring self-expression. Every year, people get decked out in scales, body paint, hand-crafted bikinis, and crazy headwear. Some go for realistic mermaid and merman (MER-MAN!) getups, while others throw convention to the wind and go absolutely ape shit. The parade attracts hundreds of thousands of participants, and its elaborate floats roll along through the neighborhood and the Coney Island boardwalk. A king and queen are chosen every year, and awards are given for best float, music group, and costume. After the freak show subsides, the train ride back is full of glitter, fake fish scales, and half-naked merpeople.

NATHAN'S FAMOUS HOT DOG EATING CONTEST
#PukeFest
1310 Surf Avenue

The famous face-stuffing, stomach-curdling fest goes down every Fourth of July in front of a giant scoreboard at Nathan's. People from around the world gather to eat as many hot dogs as they can in ten minutes. The contest officially started in the early '70s to promote Nathan's and grew to massive pro-portions. Over the years, new techniques like "dunking" (where hot dogs and buns are drenched in soda right before being scarfed down) were introduced and effec-tively upped the game. Takeru Kobayashi and Joey Chestnut have been the dueling wiener champs for years, each shoving sixty to sev-enty dogs in their mouths to win the coveted "bejeweled" mustard-yellow belt. The spec-tacle is attended by thousands, and if you want to see any dog action, get there early.

5 WAYS TO PUKE AT CONEY ISLAND

Everyone knows that the party doesn't start until someone reaches for a barf bag. Turn your insides out with these combos.

CYCLONE ($9) + NATHAN'S

First, pretend you're training for the Nathan's contest and down a handful of those famous dogs, dipping the buns in your soda so they slide down your throat like migrating trout. Then drag your dog-filled gut to the Cyclone, the oldest, most rickety coaster this country has ever seen. In a matter of minutes, the Cyclone will make sure that the dogs start barking.

DENO'S WONDER WHEEL ($7) + TORTA

The Tortas at Plaza Mexico Dona Zita are huge, and Deno's wheel, a historic Ferris wheel with a twist, is wonderously nauseating. Dona Zita is right under the wheel, so giving your stomach time to settle isn't an option. Grab a chorizo torta ($8), a spicy sandwich stuffed to max capacity, with a side of *elote*, Mexican street corn slathered in mayo and funky cheese. If you go for a swinging car, there's no way all that grub is staying inside of you.

SLINGSHOT ($20) + TOTONNO'S

Totonno's is a destination pizza joint that won't let you buy just one slice. Scarf the entire pie, loaded with deliciously greasy pepperoni, and set that ball of dough into motion on the Slingshot, a ride with a very literal name. You'll get into a spherical cage attached to bouncy strings with a brave friend and be flung into the air, letting gravity settle the rest.

ELECTRO SPIN ($6) + EGG CREAM

A Brooklyn egg cream is, ironically, made with just milk and seltzer, stirred vigorously until it's thick and frothy. Down one of these fast at Tom's Restaurant, the Coney outpost of BK's legendary diner, then hop on the Electro Spin to stir things up even further. The ride begins slowly, swaying up and down, but eventually rolls into a death spin that'll no doubt turn you into a human soda fountain.

FUN FACT

Brooklyn's famous egg creams actually have no eggs or cream. A scammy way for a soda syrup company to raise revenue, two dudes in Crown Heights decided to create a fountain drink that was frothy enough to contain expensive eggs and cream but actually had neither.

BROOKLYN FLYER ($6) + FREAK BAR

The Freak Bar (1208 Surf Avenue) is a new addition to Coney off the main drag and usually opens at noon. Get in there early and check out the cool designs while downing freak show-labeled beers like the Sword Swallower and Mermaid Pilsner. When you're good and drunk on the witch's brew, jump on the Brooklyn Flyer, a demonic version of a carousel where you sit in a plastic, chain-suspended seat that will eventually lift you up about 100 feet over Coney Island while rotating to give you a 360-degree view from the top. Your feet will dangle, and the booze will want out.

OTP Tip: Head back to the Freak Bar at night for round two. Ten dollars buys you entry into the Coney Island Circus Sideshow where you'll see fire-eaters, sword-swallowers, and a bunch of freak people you'll probably befriend on your subway ride home.

BONUS

Eat some funnel cake from Paul's Daughter with a side of clams on the half shell and ask Zoltar how long until it all comes funneling back up.

The ride out to Coney Island can get long and boring. Go ahead and jump that train to explore the neighborhoods along the way.

GRAVESEND
(F Train Stop: Avenue X)
Next stop: old-school pizza!

Go to L&B Spumoni Gardens (2725 86th Street) when you're in the mood for a carefree carbfest. This tourist attraction of a restaurant was first conceived as a spumoni (Italian layered ice cream) stand, but the place took off in another direction. While their spumoni is pretty damn good, the famous thing here is the Sicilian pie. This kind of pizza is a little different than what you're used to. The huge square pie is made with a superthick and chewy crust that's first covered in cheese (to allow it to melt into the dough), then doused in sauce. None of this dainty thin-crust business; L&B Sicilian pie is fully loaded and more like a fluffy pizza cake. The whole place is very welcoming and feels like your grandmother's house after school. The décor is gaudy Italian, and while there's a bunch of Italian classics on the menu, stick to the Sicilian and finish off with brightly colored pistachio spumoni.

SHEEPSHEAD BAY
(B Train Stop: Sheepshead Bay)
Next stop: seafood and beef

Hop off at Sheepshead Bay for a few and throw back some legendary seafood and roast beef. You'll get a gold star if you can drag your ass back up to the train platform after all is said and eaten.

SEAFOOD LEGENDS

JORDAN'S LOBSTER DOCK
#FreshLobster #outdoor
3165 Harkness Avenue

Both a restaurant and retail fish market, Jordan's has been laying down the lobster since 1938. The prices are up there, but we're talkin' lobster and you shouldn't be comfortable eating it cheap. Jordan's has great clams and oysters, but maintain your focus and head to the tank. Pick a lobster, have them steam it, and take that critter for a walk to the outdoor seating area.

RANDAZZO'S CLAM BAR
#seafood #LocalFavorite
2017 Emmons Avenue

An old-school Sicilian seafood institution, this place is famous for two things: the cutest nonna in the world, Helen Randazzo, and the super-slow-cooked tomato sauce she labored over. While Helen is unfortunately no longer here, her sauce remains and is best sampled over the shrimp or lobster fra diavolo (hot). Don't worry about the décor, and eat the giant portions with your hands. We've heard mixed reviews about Randazzo's now that Helen is no longer at the helm, but either way, it's a place that remains close to the locals' seafood-lovin' hearts.

BAY BREAK

The actual bay is a great place to take a casual stroll (especially after pounding your weight in seafood), eavesdrop on Russian lady conversations, and watch the standing water attract hydrophilic birds like ducks and swans. The topography is flatter than you're used to in more bustling parts of Brooklyn, and a little bridge connects the commercial and residential areas. Check out the Holocaust Memorial at the west end of the bay and have a seat on a bench to think things through.

ROAST BEEF BATTLE
ROLL-N-ROASTER VERSUS BRENNAN & CARR

Brooklynites love to argue about food, and these two can stand up to a heated roast beef battle. We're not sure which one takes the beef cake, but here are some stats to help you figure out which sandwich you'll grace with your grip.

	ROLL-N-ROASTER	**BRENNAN & CARR**
Years in Biz	40+	75+
The Beef	made to desired temperature; sliced thin; and dripping with jus	pink and tender; size of an ottoman; double-dipped with jus on the side so you can do you
Best Sidekick	sweet and crispy corn fritters	cheese fries
Décor	a relic from a decade that believed roast beef sandwiches were diet food	clean with lots of wood and brick
Gimmick	love wall	ancient meat grinder
Price	$4.45	$5.50

RUSSIAN FOOD

BRIGHTON BEACH

(B Train Stop: Brighton Beach)
Next stop: Mother Russia says eat!

If you've ever wondered what it's like to stroll around the former USSR, Brighton Beach is the closest thing you'll find. Predominantly populated by immigrants from Odessa, Ukraine, Brighton Beach is filled with little old ladies who want nothing more out of life than to feed you. Heavy on meat, potatoes, cabbage, and beets, here's what babushka is planning to shove down your throat.

PIROSHKI

Handheld fried dough balls, these are bigger than your average doughnut hole and come stuffed with a big helping of homey ingredients like ground meat, potatoes, and slightly sour cabbage. In front of Tokyo Bay (which isn't even remotely Japanese) at 309 Brighton Beach Avenue, the babushkas have taken over the sidewalk, selling their freshly prepared piroshki from plastic bins. A few shops down, an old lady always hangs out of the window with her own pipin'-hot offerings for a few bucks. At the risk of pissing off any of these women, get one from each.

PELMENI

A kind of dumpling, pelmeni are little pockets of dough stuffed with meat, potatoes, or cabbage. Brighton Beach is full of pelmeni; we've even seen some petrified stragglers on the sidewalk. You can get them frozen at any market and order them up by the dozen at cafés and restaurants. At Cafe Glechik (3159 Coney Island Avenue), every $6 order is packed into a little clay pot and you have a choice between "Siberian," veal, or chicken.

PLOV

Plov is a slow-cooked rice dish that's heavily laced with gamey lamb, carrots, and sometimes dried fruit. Nargis Cafe (2818 Coney Island Avenue) is an Uzbek joint that always gets their lamb right. The space is nicely laid out with red wooden chairs and tables and colorful rugs hung on the walls (the only way all Russians like their rugs). Their plov is just $8.50 per plate and comes with tender lamb chunks on top. Uzbeks are known for being master meat grillers, and you should also get a veal liver kebab ($4.25) just in case.

BORSCHT

Perhaps the one Ukrainian dish that the world has heard of, borscht is the country's biggest source of culinary pride. In the states, the soup is often made more palatable by being run through the blender. In Ukraine, they dig the super chunk and wouldn't let an s-blade near their borscht. Packed with stain-everything beets, beef, and cabbage, this soup has had the whole nation pissing pink for eternity. Skovorodka (615 Brighton Beach Avenue) is a little pricier than the dive joints in the area but is worth it.

FUN FACT

Not all borscht is beet red. Green borscht, made with spinach, omits beets altogether and is a milder, brothier soup often consumed during the not-so-frigid months. Skovorodka's got you covered on that one too.

SALAT OLIVIER

Ukrainians don't fuck with leafy greens when it comes to salads. Their bunny food comes fully loaded with meat, mayo, and an array of chunky vegetables, and olivier is the heaviest of the spread. A thick concoction of potatoes, eggs, ham, and peas held together with a bucket of mayo, got yours at Brighton Bazaar (1007 Brighton Beach Avenue), where all of your eating dreams come to life. The whole place is loaded with tin lowboys, overflowing with pickled things, salads, and veggies. There are also meats, smoked fish, Russian candy bins, a ridiculous amount of sausages, breads, and pastries. Everything behind the counter is sold by weight. You will never leave this store voluntarily.

OTP Tip: Don't leave without stocking up on Baltika (No. 5 or No. 9); it's the best Russian beer there is.

NAPOLEON

Not a small Frenchman, but a cake that'll make you wish your mouth took up more of your face. The classic version contains at least fifteen layers of flaky dough layered with gobs of creamy custard. The one at Taste of Russia (219 Brighton Beach Avenue) is served up by the pound, and when you request one slice, they give you a giant rectangle that'll be hard to carry.

VODKA AND ZAKUSKI

Ukrainians believe that no meal is complete without a hundred grams of vodka, paired with a bite of food (*zakuski*) to help the booze reach its destination more smoothly. *Zakuski* can be anything from cold cuts to *blini* (mini-pancakes) with sour cream and caviar. Most commonly, people chase shots with something pickled (tomatoes, cauliflower, carrots, mushrooms, peppers, garlic root, and herring). Cafe Euroasia (602 Brighton Beach Boulevard, on 6th Street) is pretty much like a college cafeteria, but this place is BYO vodka and has all the right accompanying side dishes for super low prices (tongue salad, anyone?). The waitresses are surly Russian women, and you'll be blasted with weird Russian pop music from the '80s. The drunk patrons add a nice touch to the experience.

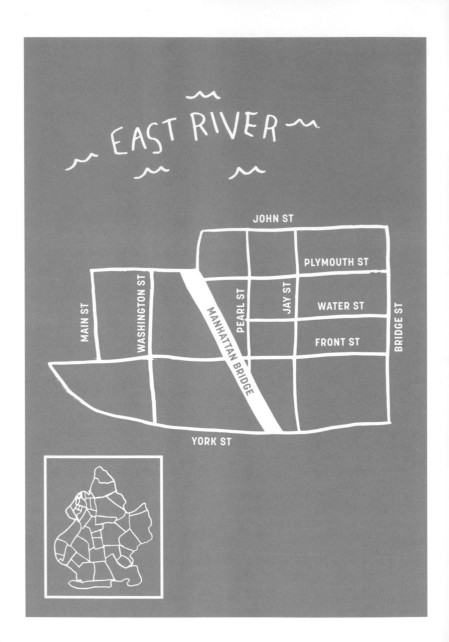

DUMBO

A ridiculous acronym (Down Under the Manhattan Brooklyn Overpass) for a quirky little spot on the BK map. Just one stop (or, twenty-minute walk) from Manhattan, DUMBO has a unique vantage point of the iconic NYC skyline, with the underbelly of the Brooklyn Bridge cutting through the scenery. Although DUMBO is mostly business, the kind of business that happens here isn't a nine-to-five stress bubble. From architects to Busta Rhymes, many creative professionals hold down offices (and a few residences) in DUMBO, and when they need a break, they head down to the newly renovated Brooklyn Bridge Park (complete with a historic carousel), or pop into Brooklyn Roasting Company on the water's edge, where mind-jolting espresso shots kick work into high gear. For a small section of Brooklyn, DUMBO has a lot to offer.

COFFEE AND BAKERIES

BROOKLYN ROASTING COMPANY
#coffee #IndustrialChic
25 Jay Street

Come to Brooklyn Roasting to taste their hard, strong labor of love. Relative newcomers to the NYC coffee scene, BRC blew up in a big way and for good reason. You can almost taste the elbow grease these guys put into making their coffee. They source their beans from interesting places (like one of our favorite backpacking destinations: Chiapas, Mexico), roast them right in front of your face, and spread their seed by supplying coffeehouses all over the city. Entering the shop feels like stepping into a weathered French press, with repurposed metal and wood chunks making up their seating and waiting areas and the smell of coffee permeating every crevice.

 # EAT

GRIMALDI'S

#pizza #legend #TouristFood
1 Front Street

A pizza joint that gained worldwide fame, Grimaldi's has been firing up its twenty-five-ton, hand-built, coal-burning oven for several decades. While the ownership has changed hands and spin-off locations opened in various parts of the city, the original location is where all the tourists flock to stand in line (as no reservations are taken) for hours to stuff their faces with a full pie (it's not sold by the slice). Sure, a lot of it is hype and any local will tell you there are better pizza options available, but Grimaldi's is legendary and unique in its own right, with simple ingredients, perfectly charred thin crust, and that smoky coal oven flavor that nobody can replicate.

JULIANA'S PIZZA

#pizza #RealGrimaldis
19 Old Fulton Street

While Grimaldi's is a tourist attraction, Juliana's is where people go to just eat. Patsy Grimaldi and his coal-fired oven are what made Grimaldi's a pizza legend in Brooklyn. Here's a little well-known secret: Patsy and the oven are at Juliana's, not Grimaldi's (which changed ownership and moved up the street a few years back). If you're looking for the real-deal pizza sensation, it's at Juliana's. While the tourists starve in line, break yourself off a piece of delicious, perfectly charred pie. A classic Margherita is all you need to get an idea of why Patsy has withstood the test of time.

FUN FACT

Grimaldi's was actually supposed to be in Manhattan. Since setting up new coal ovens in the city was illegal at the time, Patsy opened his shop under the Brooklyn Bridge where his famous oven could burn legally.

 SEE AND DO

BROOKLYN BRIDGE

#historic #views

Completed in 1883, the Brooklyn Bridge is one of the oldest suspension bridges in the country and, along with San Fran's Golden Gate, one of the most iconic. An important link between Brooklyn and Manhattan, the bridge is partly responsible for the development of Brooklyn into the densely populated, diverse borough it is today. If you walk it from the Brooklyn side, the feeling you get when the Manhattan skyline appears as you near the middle of the bridge is indescribable. You feel small, big, alive, and elated. Take this walk twice (once during the day, then at night) to get the full effect and remember to stay on the pedestrian path (or prepare to be yelled at/hit by the bikers flying through).

BROOKLYN BRIDGE PARK

#waterfront #ManhattanViews #carousel

Wrapped around the DUMBO waterfront, facing the financial district of lower Manhattan and winding down under the Brooklyn Bridge, this park had a facelift a few years back and is lookin' mighty fine. A nicely laid-out stretch of park, the space's curvaceous walkways lead you through some gorgeous points of interest. Following the east entrance of the park, you'll hit a rocky little shore where you can hide out with your lunch near the water, or opt for a higher-up perch on the open grassy field in the middle. The stairs right beneath the field offer a front-and-center view of the city and are an awesome spot to stare into the concrete jungle as the water crashes against the stairs during high tide. Following the path, you'll come across dilapidated warehouse buildings on your left and a carousel up ahead. The further you walk, the newer (and more touristy) the surroundings get, with a lookout point, mod benches, and a café among the trees making up the park atmosphere. The Fulton Ferry docks nearby, so you can take a ride across the river to switch up your mode of transport. During the summer, this park is filled with ice-cream vendors, festivals, outdoor movies, and weekday photo shoots (some are models, some are bridezillas).

OTP Tip: If you're at the waterfront on Sunday, you'll find Smorgasburg at Pier 5 where a hundred food vendors vie for your taste buds.

FUN FACTS

While the Brooklyn Bridge is now free to cross, when it first opened, the toll was a penny per person and a nickel per cow.

If you ever decide to climb atop the cables of the Brooklyn Bridge, know that there are falcons that nest up there. Fucking falcons!

BROOKLYN NAVY YARD

#landmark #AbandonedBuildings
BLDG 92, 63 Flushing Avenue

This industrial park was an active navy ship-yard and played major roles in every war on American soil. Innovations in shipbuilding, scientific developments, the blocking of slave trade, and some popular naval catastrophes all happened on these docks during the yard's two-hundred-year history. You can still look at the creepy old military housing through peepholes in barriers set up along Flushing Avenue. Currently, the docks are used by various manufacturers, artisans, and producers, notably the Steiner Studios, a movie production studio that recently partnered with Brooklyn College to create a film program that gives students a hands-on experience previously only available in Hollywood. You can learn about this area's rich history in BLDG 92, a multi-faceted exhibit space that also showcases the works of the Navy Yard's current tenants.

DUMBO ARTS FESTIVAL

#OutdoorArt #GreatViews

A free, outdoor, three-day event that showcases the best in Brooklyn art, this festival is a giant conglomerate of local and international independent artists of all disciplines. With the underbelly of the Brooklyn Bridge as the backdrop, artists pull out their best works and display large-scale installations, murals, sculptures, and performance pieces around the already picturesque neighborhood. Street dancers, poets, and visual artists occupy every cobblestoned corner, and visitors spill out into the adjacent and newly renovated Brooklyn Bridge Park, where you glimpse into the arts of Brooklyn and lay around staring off into the Manhattan skyline from the best vantage point in Brooklyn.

VINEGAR HILL

#GhostTown #UrbanHike

Nearby Vinegar Hill is one of the weirdest places in Brooklyn. If you walk away from the bridge on John Street you'll be taken to what looks like a ghost village, with disheveled store fronts and broken sidewalks. It may look abandoned, but the place is a thriving community with a huge mansion (the former residence of the navy colonel) looming at the top of the hill.

SHOP

JACQUES TORRES CHOCOLATE

#truffles #HotChocolate #IceCream
#FamousFood
66 Water Street

Regarded as some sort of chocolate mecca, Jacques Torres's OG shop is on Water Street. Not to be giant snobs, but we've had better chocolate. This place has a huge tourist draw, and the prices are high. But the décor of both shops, bright and chandeliered, will put you in the chocolate-eating mood, and the truffles are pretty and come in a variety of flavors that change frequently. They also sell giant cookies and other chocolate-covered edibles. There are two reasons we'd haul ass to Jacques Torres: When it's freezing outside, their thick hot chocolate is like someone wrapped a bear around your insides and, during the unbearable NYC summer, Jacques's adjacent ice-cream shop really hits the spot.

THE POWERHOUSE ARENA

#bookstore #CoolTitles #events
37 Main Street

Powerhouse, an independent publisher, is very selective about the titles they carry, and if you're looking for what's cool in lit, this is the place to go. Here, you'll find large-format coffee table books and neatly arranged hip-hop-heavy titles. A massive open space that isn't cluttered with books, the store sits on a cobblestone street right by the water. Powerhouse isn't all words either. They hold cool events, like art openings, lectures, and other promotional events with free wine and snack receptions.

SINGULARITY & CO.

#bookstore #SciFi #NerdParadise
18 Bridge Street

Owned by a quirky husband-and-wife team, this hidden bookshop will make you revisit your awkward, sci-fi-loving high school years. The store's shelves are jam-packed with vintage science fiction and fantasy novels that'll stir your imagination. The owners are dedicated to reviving the dying genre in any way they can. Every month, they "rescue" an out-of-print book from SaveTheSciFi.com by publishing it themselves. Whether you're still a big science nerd or just appreciate the genre, Singularity & Co. is a unique place to visit when exploring the surrounding creepery of Vinegar Hill.

PARTYING

SUPERFINE

#bar #FreePool #SkinnyFries
126 Front Street

Channeling a funky, circusy vibe in a more upscale(ish) setting, Superfine is a good spot to grab a drink and soak up the atmosphere, which consists of dimly lit corners, an extensive winding bar, and industrial lighting. While they have a full kitchen with decent food, the best time to eat here is on Sunday during the live bluegrass brunch. Otherwise, we suggest sticking to drinks and pool. (The table's in the front. It's free; your break.)

TREAT YOURSELF

From DUMBO, hike up to Brooklyn Heights and treat yourself to . . .

THE BEST VIEW

Only the oldest and richest of Brooklyn can afford to live here, but walking around and absorbing the scenery doesn't come with a mortgage payment. Gaze into the old, ornate bay windows of the wealthy as you make your way to the Brooklyn Heights Promenade, which offers you the most incredible view of the NYC skyline at eye level. Little benches are set up along the walkway overlooking the water, and you can sit and absorb the city while Lady Liberty stands in the distance. The promenade culminates near the Brooklyn Bridge, so you can take a fifteen-minute hike across to the city you've been admiring from afar.

THE GAMIEST MEAT

Henry's (44 Henry Street) is cooking up weird meats, and not just for shock value. They're experts in wild game and know exactly what to do with elk, turtle, and wild boar. All of their meats are sourced locally, and they've been searing, braising, and coaxing flavor out of all kinds of edible ani-mals for more than forty years. The interior is a little old-school with no fancy modern décor. Just cozy brick, nice lighting, and comfortable seating. If you're going down the meat rabbit hole, there is an entire wild game menu to choose from, which includes succulent game hen, rich wild boar belly, and their popular herb-crusted elk chop, among others. Their wine list is one of the best in Brooklyn and the twenty-one-crêpe dessert is insane.

SOMETHING SUPER WEIRD

The brownstone located at 58 Joralemon Street looks like an average residence, but it's actually totally fake. The building is used as a metro ventilator and houses subway rails.

HOURS OF FOOD-BROWSING ENTERTAINMENT

A favorite local "ethnic" foods store, Sahadi's Importing Company (187 Atlantic Avenue) has all kinds of interesting things that'll keep your eyes entertained for hours. Best known for their selection of spices and nuts, Sahadi's has a bulk section that feels like an outdoor market somewhere in the Middle East, with familiar nuts, dried fruit, spices you've never heard of, and ancient grains all scooped and weighed per your request. There is a pickle and olive bar with things like pickled baby eggplants and huge, colorful olives, all for a really great price. Their prepared food, found in several areas at the back of the store, is something truly unique. With more than thirty dishes on rotation, they do kebabs, grain and veggie salads, creamy hummus, and homey sides, and they have a separate stand for flatbreads. Charlie Sahadi regularly hangs out on the floor and, despite their enormous popularity, is always in a good mood and willing to help you select something tasty from the store's abundance of edibles.

WORLD FAMOUS CHEESECAKE

So Junior's (386 Flatbush Avenue) isn't technically in Brooklyn Heights, but suck it up and walk . . . this is famous cheesecake! The standard by which other New York cheesecakes are judged, this mom-and-pop joint keeps it all about traditional, stop-your-heart creaminess. Their cheesecake is rich, dosed out in a portion you'd be ashamed to eat alone, and comes in all kinds of flavors.

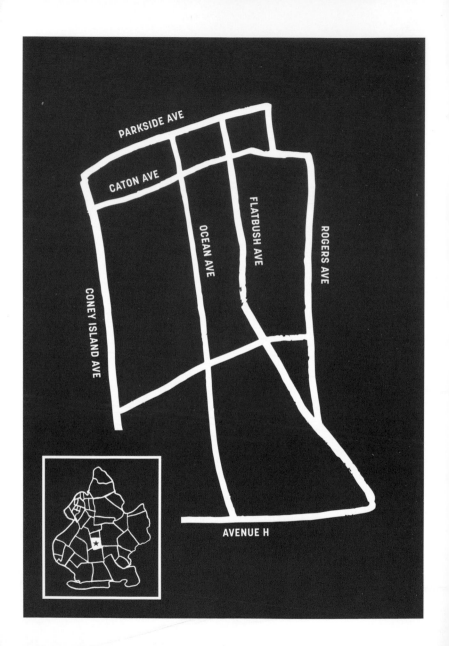

FLATBUSH/ DITMAS PARK

Flatbush is an interesting mash-up of cultures and has been inhabited by an array of immigrants, namely Italians, Jews, Africans, and Haitians—all of whom have left a mark on the hood's character. Flatbush has a huge West Indian community, with their spicy Caribbean flare, and while some places may seem a little intimidating, you'll find unique regional dishes that are normally only available on the islands. On the other end of the spectrum, destination restaurants and cocktail bars have sprung up on Cortelyou Road, and they continue to draw top city chefs into their kitchens. For baseball fans, Flatbush is also historically relevant as it was the home of Ebbets Field, where the former Brooklyn Dodgers used to play. Di Fara sits in nearby Midwood and is worth the trip this "deep" into Brooklyn.

COFFEE AND BAKERIES

QATHRA
#coffee #FreshDécor #lunch
1112 Cortelyou Road

Qathra is a monster of a coffee shop that also has amazing lunch fare. Dimly lit and full of wood, brick, and plants, Qathra will make you feel like a foraging squirrel. Here, your rodent heart can feast on freshly made pastries (the almond croissants are amazing), Counter Culture Coffee, and a good selection of breakfast and lunch sandwiches and salads. Take your pickings to their backyard, which is a nice extension of the woodsy interior. They don't do laptops on weekends, so bring a book.

FUN FACT

Ebinger's Baking Co., the creator of the infamous "Brooklyn Blackout Cake," went bankrupt in 1972 after almost a hundred years of business. The abandoned building still stands at 1898 Flatbush Avenue. While many have tried to recreate the cake over the years, the true recipe died with the bakery and remains a mystery to this day.

EAT

CAFE TIBET
#TibetanFood #BYOB
1510 Cortelyou Road

As far as holes-in-the-walls go, Cafe Tibet is a unique little hut that'll entice you with its unfamiliar cuisine and low prices. The menu is pretty extensive, with items you recognize and others you'll have to ask about. The staff is happy to guide you into your comfort zone, and the décor is warm and charming. Start it off with the beef momo (Tibet's take on a dumpling) and continue the climb to their pork chili, which comes with tingmo (a steamed bread). The service is a few notches slower than the NYC usual, but the place is BYOB so you can sip on your beer while you wait.

MIMI'S HUMMUS
#hummus
1209 Cortelyou Road

You thought you knew hummus, but Mimi will prove you dead-wrong. For some reason, hers is just better than that chickpea sludge you've been munching. Here, you'll want to get fancy with it and order the mushroom hummus ($9), a smooth and creamy dip that comes with a flavorful heap of mushrooms, two pitas, and some pickles. With the exception of the Israeli salad, the rest of the menu is just OK and gets a little pricey.

the BEST WEST indian FOOD LIVES HERE

Flatbush has a dense Caribbean population, hailing from Jamaica, Trinidad, Haiti, Guyana, and all the tiny islands bobbing nearby, and it serves up some of the most authentic food around. West Indian food (aka Caribbean) is an insane combo of flavors influenced by Africa, India, Europe, and China, with hints of others. Here's a rundown of a few West Indian dishes and the best grab-and-go spots to get them.

DOUBLES

The weird name suggests you're going to get two of something, and that's never a bad thing. The ultimate Trini street food, doubles are two pieces of fried bara (bread) traditionally stuffed with curried chickpeas, tangy tamarind paste, and sometimes hot pepper. These are eaten mostly for breakfast. Oatmeal ain't got shit on doubles!

Bake and Things (1489 Flatbush Avenue) kills it on doubles. They're $1.50, the channa (chickpea) filling is luscious, and you sauce it yourself. Throw in an aloo pie (potato pastry) for two bucks and you're good to go.

Bonus: If you find yourself in Bed-Stuy still craving doubles, A&A Bake & Doubles (481 Nostrand Avenue) is amazing for these little Trini sandwiches, which will also set you back $1.50. Get there before 3:00 p.m.; otherwise, no doubles for you.

JERK

For the flavor whores out there, Jamaican jerk is perhaps the most mouth-pleasing flavor you'll ever find. A mix of more spices than your rack can handle (with Scotch bonnets providing the kick), jerk seasoning is a dry rub applied to proteins before they hit the heat. Many meats can be jerked, but chicken is the classic, and Peppa's (738 Flatbush Avenue) jerks her chicken with vigor. Peppa's began as a street stand called Danny and Pepper's, but the two split and Peppa's is the pickup joint that survived the drama. This chicken is rubbed down with seasoning and spice that'll dropkick every one of your taste buds. Peppa's doesn't mess around when it comes to portion size either; unless you're pregnant with octuplets, stick to the $6 small and get it with the $1 festival (bread) to tame the flames.

PATTIES

Not naked burgers, but flattened balls of meat or vegetables, patties are first seasoned and wrapped in dough, then fried. They're a common street food in many Caribbean countries like Guyana and are most popular in Jamaica. Jamaican Pride Bakery (731 Flatbush Avenue) is the patty jam. The beef patties will run you a mere $1.50. The flavorful, moist beef inside is wrapped in a flaky thin crust, and for a buck fifty, you can afford to shove many more patties in the pie hole. The place is pretty divey and easy to miss.

If your feet can't carry you around this part of the Caribbean, dollar vans are privately owned transportation vehicles that have been running along Flatbush Avenue (and many other transit-deprived areas of Brooklyn and beyond) for eternity. It won't be comfortable, it's semi-illegal, but when you need a ride, the dollar van will get you there . . . for $2.

OLD BAKU
#AzerbaijaniFood #grungy #authentic
115 Ditmas Avenue

Old Baku will be the one spot that will pump you full of so much good food that the grime factor won't matter. Serving real Azerbaijani food, unedited to fit American palettes, Old Baku is heavy on the offal, and the servers speak little English. For the middle-grounder, the best thing to try is any of their kebabs (or the $32 BBQ platter, which will stuff about four people to the gills with meat). For the ballsy, they've got testicles on the menu if you look hard enough. Their idea of salad is whole vegetables on a plate, which may be wrong but is oh-so-great. The patio out back, where you'll find old dudes clinking dominoes and chain-smoking, is the most conducive to enjoying your food adventure.

THE DOGWOOD
#BBQ #CarolinasStyle
1021 Church Avenue

Two Southern food fanatics opened up this joint in 2013 in the interest of bringing the flavor of the Carolinas to NYC. While they do some twists on the classics, none of it is that modern Southern that leaves you hungry and broke. They've got biscuits, fried chicken, pimento cheese, really good hand-cut fries, shrimp and grits, and a big juicy ($15) burger. There's an entire wall of windows for passersby to watch you go down on some good Southern cookin'.

THE FARM ON ADDERLEY
#NewAmerican #TreatYourself #FamousFood
1108 Cortelyou Road

One of Brooklyn's most popular destination restaurants, this out-of-the-way place attracts swarms of Manhattanites who normally only travel this far into Brooklyn for something solid. In an area known more for McChicken than confit, with its meticulously procured ingredients, the Farm brought with it a certain level of sophistication that's on par with the fancy stuff available in the city. Some call that food snobbery; we just think it tastes good. While they do serve up a mean burger (for $14), we like to funnel our funds into their steak, medium-rare with a side of Brussels sprouts. Their portions are hearty and the brunch menu (the custardy French toast!) never disappoints. The Farm isn't cheap, but they have a little annex café/bakery in the area called Nine Chains where all the beggars (us!) go to get a taste of the good life.

WHEATED
#FancyPizza #whiskey
905 Church Avenue

Despite naming themselves Wheated, which sounds like getting painfully beaten with old bread, this fancy pizza spot is doing a lot of things right. The unique thing about their Neapolitan-style pizza is its sourdough crust, a tangy ordeal that crisps up well in the oven and can handle a topping pileup. Each of their pizzas is named after a nearby neighborhood, and their house cocktails are superb. While they aren't very overt with hitting food stereotypes (c'mon, why aren't beets on the Brighton Beach?), the pies are fantastic, with an extensive vegan and white-pie selection, and the special Red Hook, with its mortadella and pistachios, is super good. Each pie ($10-$15) is thin and perfect for one and pairs well with whiskey (because what doesn't?).

DI FARA

Di Fara (1424 Avenue J) is the only reason you will go out to Midwood. Locals will agree that this pizza joint captures the essence of famed New York–style pizza like no other touristy place in any travel guide to this fair city. The guy behind the oven (Dom DeMarco) has been there tossing his dough and spreading his sauce exactly the same perfect way for more than fifty years. His simple, super-Italian approach to pizza has won Di Fara a lot of praise throughout the years. The menu isn't jumbled with a bunch of crap; just a few familiar toppings and the option of a regular or square slice (or whole pie). The crust is perfectly thin and bubbly, charred in spots like it should be. The sauce is sweet and tart, and laid out in just the right amount. The cheese is stretchy, gooey, and not too greasy. Di Fara achieves that hard-to-nail sauce-to-cheese ratio that every pizza snob raves about. This pizza is magical, and while it's not cheap, nor conveniently located, it's worth every penny and mile traveled.

SEE AND DO

BROOKLYN BANYA

#RussianBath #EucalyptusBeating #food
#BYOVodka

602 Coney Island Avenue

While you'd expect this place to be right in the middle of Brighton Beach, it's steaming the shit out of Flatbush instead. Although it does take it down a notch to attract Americans, just because you take the banya out of Brighton doesn't mean you can take the Brighton out of the banya. An all-day experience, you come to get awkwardly undressed with coed strangers (or bring friends and get naked with them), steam yourself purple in the hot sauna and cool off in the pool, drink vodka ($4 shots or BYOB), smoke cigs on the roof, and eat until your pores smell like meat, cheese, and dough. You'll see people walking around with eucalyptus brooms, and if you're lucky, you'll get a good beating.

PARTYING

Sycamore

HIGHBURY PUB

#bar #soccer

1002 Cortelyou Road

This is one of the only places we've ever been that doesn't play music. While it may feel like an echo tunnel of awkward at first, it does force you to strike up conversation. You didn't come all the way to Brooklyn to keep your mouth shut, and Highbury will get that small talk out of you one drink at a time. A soccer pub owned by an Irishman, this joint has a healthy happy hour where drafts are $5 until 7:00 p.m. daily.

SYCAMORE

#bar #florist #whiskey #backyard

1118 Cortelyou Road

Many bars work hard to think of some sort of gimmick to draw the drinkers in their direction, but Sycamore went a step further. It's not just set up like a fake flower shop; they're actually a full-service florist (like with bouquets and shit). Sycamore throws fun parties and lets you bring whatever you want to grill in the flowery yard when the weather's right. They've got plenty of dark liquor (largest selection of whiskey we've seen) to make you feel like a true gentleman, fragrant roses to make you feel like a lady, and vice versa.

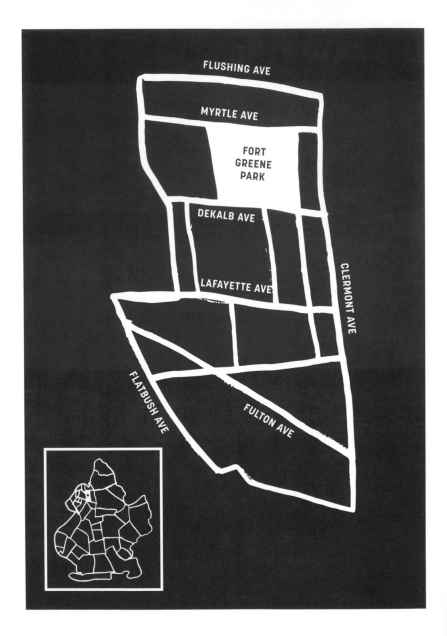

FORT GREENE

People pay the big bucks to live here, but even if you don't visit any of Fort Greene's wine bars or gastro-tasty pubs, just walking the wide, tree-lined, elaborate brownstone-littered streets is a bay-window-gawking experience. The summer means this hood is in full bloom, with people drinking wine on stoops and eating al fresco. On the flipside, winter snow collects on the ornate churches, gargoyles, structures, and stoop rails, making Fort Greene look like a painting.

COFFEE AND BAKERIES

SMOOCH
#coffee #wine #vegemite
264 Carlton Street

Perhaps the only café bold enough to sell vegemite, this Aussie-owned establishment fits into its Brownstone Belt location well. Everything they offer is organic, from daytime coffee to nighttime wine. The best seat in the house is to the left of the entrance, up one step and on the cow-upholstered bench with matching backboard. The food is standard café fare, nothing too interesting, with a good amount of vegetarian options. This place gets a little hippie at times, and the baristas are sometimes so laid-back that they may as well be sleeping. If the weather's right, there is plenty of seating curbside on the tree benches, and if the yoga moms aren't around to kill your quiet, it can be a peaceful retreat.

WTF COFFEE LABS
#espresso #ExtractionContraptions
47 Willoughby Avenue

By far the geekiest coffee establishment around, WTF Coffee Labs has hoarded every coffee contraption known to man to give you the option of drinking your coffee either pulled through a siphon, pressed through a French press, bloomed in a pour over (or Chemex), strained through a sock pot, finagled through an AeroPress, or cold-brewed. You also get options when it comes to beans. The baristas here are well aware of how pretentious all this sounds and will help you out should you get stuck. The place is small, but curbside seating is great on a nice day. If you've ventured deep into the nerdy world of specialty coffee brewing, this place will stroke your need for bean.

🍔 EAT

MADIBA RESTAURANT
#SouthAfrican #TreatYourself
#FancyVagabondDécor
195 DeKalb Avenue

Come here for weird meats and not-yet-Americanized South African cuisine. Tastefully colorful, with Mandela memorabilia, a coke bottle chandelier, beautiful African tapestries, and rustic seating, Madiba is set against the backdrop of Fort Greene's historic brownstones. A place dedicated to bringing the shebeen (or a dining hall that offers respite to weary travelers) experience to the States, Madiba is all about promoting unity and togetherness with their unique cuisine (also, some of their earnings are fed back into charities in South Africa). Named after Nelson Mandela's nickname, Madiba serves creative food that would have made the man proud. Ostrich carpaccio, bunny chow (bread bowls filled with chunky curries), bobotie (a baked meat and egg dish), and spiced-up sauces (like—take a breath—the monkey-gland sauce). The outdoor seating feels like you're dining in a faraway jungle while elbow-rubbing with Brooklyn's finest.

BLACK IRIS
#MiddleEastern #BYOB
228 Dekalb Avenue

A good sit down joint that nails everything you love about Middle Eastern food and allows you to bring in your own booze to sweeten the deal. As for the basics, Black Iris knows its way around a creamy hummus and baba ghanoush and crisps up its falafel just right. Their pita bread is freshly baked to fluffy, chewy perfection and is showcased as the crust for their wide selection of not so American "pitzaas." Black Iris' well-spiced leg of lamb and Merguez sausage entrées will help you dig deeper into Mid East cuisine. Pop in with a six pack and an appetite.

OLEA
#Mediterranean #Sexy
171 Lafayette Avenue

When the sun sets, the lights inside Olea flicker and the pillowed-window seats will lure you in to sit, drink, eat, and play footsie all night. Olea serves dishes from across the Mediterranean with Turkey, Greece, and Spain all inventively represented on the menu. While most people go here for brunch (their Turkish breakfast and Bloody Mary are top-notch), we like the ambiance and thinner crowd during dinner, where you can make a meal of several tapas like flavorful Greek meatballs, fried haloumi cheese that sits on a tangy bed of romesco, and hangar steak soaked in sangria. Olea's seafood paella is one of the best we've had outside of Espana herself. Also, if you're in the mood for a quickie, Olea doesn't mind if you just hit it and quit it at the bar.

 SEE AND DO

BAM
#theater #movies #shows
Peter Jay Sharp Building (main)
30 Lafayette Avenue

The mega performing arts center of Brooklyn, BAM is comprised of several complexes that put on high-caliber performances (plays, movies, concerts, dance shows, and a bunch more) at reasonable prices. The Harvey Theater is where all the play action goes down. From Shakespeare to reinterpretations of Shakespeare to modern works, the theater is fully equipped to give you a Broadway-esque experience. Smaller productions are held in their Fishman space. The Rose Cinemas is the movie house, and they'll put on more artsy films than your average cineplex. They've also got this kick-ass terrace and various other venues to hold just about any kind of performance.

OTP Tip: Check out BAM's Next Wave Festival (September to December) where local artists present their smaller-scale productions on the big stage. Performances tend to be raw and risky, but well produced and beautifully presented.

BRIC HOUSE
#shows #art #cheap
647 Fulton Street

A nonprofit organization that came together in 1979 to promote, inspire, and exhibit the creativity that flows through the diverse veins of Brooklyn's artsy residents, BRIC puts on multimedia shows that you can see for cheap (sometimes free). The newly renovated space sits right next to BAM, and it features several spaces like a theater that welcomes a variety of performance art (including dance, opera, and film), a gallery space, artist studios, a spacious café run by Hungry Ghost, and "the Stoop," a cool public space to discuss the artistic happenings at BRIC. Also, BRIC is the force behind Celebrate Brooklyn, the massive (mostly free) summer concert series at Prospect Park. Any organization that puts together a roster of artists like the Roots, Yo La Tengo, and Little Dragon is all right in our book.

FORT GREENE PARK
#park #HistoricFort #OutdoorMovies
Between DeKalb and Myrtle Avenues at Washington Park Street

Built around the historic Revolutionary War fort, Fort Greene Park is the granddaddy of Brooklyn's parks. Opened in 1847, twenty years before Prospect Park, this hilly greenery is great for jogging, lounging, and farmers' marketing on Saturdays. The Soul Summit Music Festival, which brings some interesting acts from a diverse range of genres, goes down here every Sunday from 3:00 p.m. to 8:00 p.m. in the summer. Occasionally the park will also host special low-key performances, which have seen the likes of Common and Talib Kweli. It's not very big but is still a nice place to hit the grass for a while.

SHOP

BROOKLYN FLEA
#WeekendThrifting #IndieDesigners
#FoodStalls #vintage # tchotchkes
176 Lafayette Avenue

A huge operation with a few locations around Brooklyn, we think this market has the perfect amount of fleas. During the weekends of the warmer months, this location of the Flea takes over a school parking lot in Fort Greene. The outdoor Flea experience is great, and the vendors include old guys who have been collecting weird pins and earrings for decades, mixed in with a new crowd that spends their days thinking of ironic pictures to screen print onto American Apparel shirts. You'll find cool art, bikes, boots, furniture, New York memorabilia, and vintage clothes. The Flea sticks it out in the cold for a while but eventually moves inside to a warehouse in Williamsburg, dragging all the food and other vendors with them. It's a fun experience but gets pricey if you're loose with your wallet.

GREENLIGHT BOOKSTORE
#books #CommunityStore
686 Fulton Street

All about promoting community, this store got its foot in the door of the now lucrative Fort Greene neighborhood very early in its development. Backed by donations from the locals (of the monetary and physical labor variety), the store was opened in 2009 and continues to retain its super-clean interior and new-as-a-baby birch-tree smell. The Greenlight Bookstore carries a good mix of titles and has a nice little section dedicated to the culinary arts. They also have hand-painted postcards and all kinds of little, nice neighborhoody things.

☺ ☆☆ **PARTYING**

HABANA OUTPOST
#corn #mojitos #BackyardDayParties
#OutdoorMovies
757 Fulton Street

Open only during the warmer months (starting mid-April), Habana Outpost is a unique food and drink experience. There is a full menu with many delicious offerings, but you go to Habana for two things: Mexican street corn on the cob (perfectly grilled, with slightly stinky cheese slathered thick and a bit of chili sprinkled on just right) and frozen mojitos. There are two lines, one for food and the other for just corn and drinks. When you get your order in, make your way outside to their spacious yard, and the little red truck out there will magically have your order in due time. Weekends are great because they project movies on the side wall in the yard. Habana is the kind of place you get trapped in for hours, meet a bunch of people, consume plenty of backyard adult beverages, and leave with corn still stuck all up in your teeth.

RED LANTERN BICYCLES
#BikeShop #beer #coffee #NutMilks
345 Myrtle Avenue

Wait, what? Party at a bike shop? Damn straight. This place serves up bikes, homemade milk they squeeze from some interesting nuts (pistachio!), small bites, and lowbrow booze (just beer and wine). A combo shop like this attracts all kinds of quirky locals looking to lube up one way or another. The staff is passionate about every aspect of their unique business, so the worst you can do here is have a drink with a few cool dudes.

FUN FACT
Habana Outpost is NYC's first fully solar-powered restaurant.

WHAT TO SEE

The Fort Greene location of the Brooklyn Flea can be overwhelming upon entry. Here's the basic breakdown so you can get in, browse smart, buy cool shit, eat, and leave happy.

CLOTHES

The wintertime finds are better here. The clothing vendors are mostly at the entrance and up the sides. You'll find some great deals on worn-in coats and sweaters. Leather boots are strewn throughout the flea, with a good selection right in the middle by the entrance. There are also local designers selling printed T-shirts, which are a little overpriced but can work as a good memento or gift.

KNICKKNACKS

Along the perimeter you'll find bins and tables filled with all kinds of interesting little things. Not just Grandma's buttons, the Flea has New York collectibles like old laundry-bag-clip pins. On the right side, in the middle row, you'll find sorted bins of rubber stamps, bracelet charms, and interesting random shit.

JEWELRY

The Flea is split into two categories on this one: There's that old costume stuff (mostly on the perimeter) that you can haggle over and buy in bulk, and the new, locally designed stuff (in the middle aisles and on the right side) that's still affordable but non-negotiable. These are usually nicely crafted, delicate pieces heavy on geometric forms.

DESIGNER VINTAGE

Toward the back, you'll find a bunch of cool old gowns and glasses. The price tags on these will make you crap your pants. Browse and move.

FURNITURE

Cool old benches, dressers, reclaimed wood tables, and chairs are set up in the middle of the Flea. You'll want to take them home until you realize shipping the pieces to wherever you're from is completely unreasonable on top of the already high asking price.

FOOD

You'll see all kinds of stalls in the back peddlin' their edibles. If you've got space for only one meal, grab a pupusa from the stall on the far left. Solber Pupusas is a champ in the Latin food game, and the bean-and-cheese-stuffed pupusas come with pickled onions, jalapeños, tomato sauce, crema, and a zesty slaw. OK and maybe have a doughnut from Dough.

Even if you don't come away with a single purchase, the surrounding neighborhood is great for strolling and peeping into Fort Greene's beautiful brownstone windows.

AT THE FLea

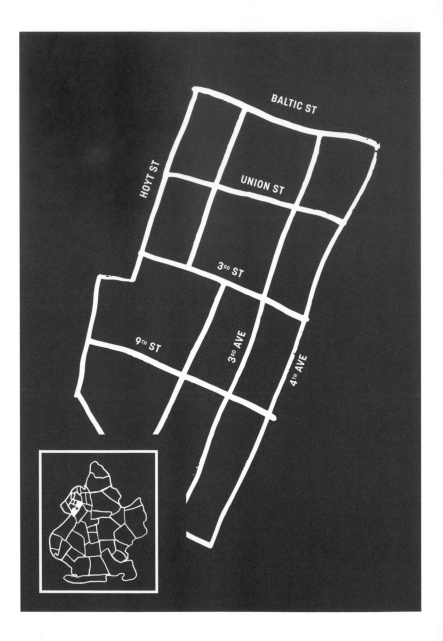

GOWANUS

Along the banks of the Gowanus Canal, or the most polluted body of water in the United States (seriously, the water is said to have STDs!) is where Brooklyn makes its big crafts. Artisans cobble things together in large warehouse workshops and make metal sculptures, furniture, specialty knives, and just about anything you can stick in a jar. Venues like the Bellhouse and Littlefield attract big names like Louis C.K. and Yo La Tengo, and hold special events like craft fairs, beer fests, and the occasional taxidermy throw-down. The industrial elbow room here provides enough space for creating some of Brooklyn's best-known wares.

COFFEE AND BAKERIES

FOUR & TWENTY BLACKBIRDS
#bakery #pie
439 3rd Avenue

The two ladies who run Brooklyn's premier pie shop love nothing more than making traditional pies kicked up a few notches with unique ingredients. The shop is tucked away from the public eye, so you can eat your pie in peace without the judgmental glances of yoga moms and stroller-jogging dads. Walking in here smells like it should, with the fresh-baked aromas of your childhood. You can go for the apple pie and you won't be disappointed. Theirs not only contains a high pile of thinly sliced, tart apples, but also a few layers of salted caramel that hug the fruit while it bakes into the perfect, luscious filling that'd make your grandma kick her oven. Other great pies include the Bittersweet Chocolate Pecan, Sweet Potato Apple Crumble, and the (giant cookie-like) Black Bottom Oat. The owners got their inspiration from their grandmothers, and you should probably get bigger pants if you're looking to taste what they're pushing here.

CROP TO CUP
#tiny #Stroopwafel
439 3rd Avenue

A small café that also serves as the company's Brooklyn office, Crop to Cup's espresso is rich and the baristas know how to handle it properly. If you have a minute to relax, pick up a Stroopwafel (a Dutch confection made by Brooklyn's Good Batch) with your hot coffee and place it on top of the cup to melt the caramel some. Get cozy at the communal table and bombard the barista with your small talk.

🍔 EAT

REYES DELI & GROCERY
#tacos #authentic
532 5th Avenue

Most delis in Brooklyn make a decent egg-and-cheese sandwich while you shop for bathroom essentials and smokes. This (not-so) secret deli has got your TP and Marlboros, but the counter hawks some of the best Mexican food around. They don't mess with frills like fusion sauces or toppings; here you get a taco ($2.25) with the bare essentials, all done right without the grease. Their salsas aren't watered down for gringos. The carnitas are as tender as baby cheeks. The quesadillas are oozing with cheese. Go here, get a torta, a six-pack while you wait, and feel like you've discovered the Mexican version of Atlantis in Gowanus.

RUNNER & STONE
#bakery #lunch #DuckPastrami
532 5th Avenue

While Runner & Stone is best known for expertly baked bread and pastries, we're all about their lunch menu, which features sandwiches and salads accented by pieces of their wonderful bread. The best item on the menu is the duck pastrami salad ($9), a well composed dish of fatty duck that comes with a tangy beer-mustard dressing and is generously sprinkled with their homemade rye croutons. Pop a few of their financiers ($1.50 each) for a smooth finish.

PILLAGE WHOLE FOODS

WHOLE FOODS MARKET

You're likely familiar with the countrywide corporate health-food megachain, but their Brooklyn location (214 3rd Street) is something a little different. After ten grueling years of jumping through hoops to appease anti–big biz locals, this Whole Foods finally got its doors open at the end of 2013. To quiet the naysayers who complained about the store competing with the local businesses, Whole Foods reached out to the hood and partnered up with every Brooklyn mom-and-pop shop within a hundred-mile radius. As such, going there for lunch means you get to taste everything Brooklyn has to offer under one big roof (with a rooftop restaurant, bar, and greenhouse).

You'll find Brooklyn fish masters Acme, whose nova lox is sliced up all buttery in the fish section; Mama O's kimchi at the salad bar; a ramen section run by Yuji Ramen; lasagna from Frankies Spuntino by weight in the prepared foods section; pies by Pie Corps; bread by neighbors Runner & Stone; and all kinds of samples from other artisanal vendors in the area. It may be right on the less-than-picturesque Gowanus Canal, but man, this place is pretty awesome.

◉ SEE AND DO

GOWANUS STUDIO SPACE
#ArtGallery #CollaborativeExhibits
166 7th Street

For artists with large ideas but limited resources, Gowanus Studio Space provides the tools necessary to create big projects. They've got wood, fabrication, and print shops, and they teach classes about relevant topics like welding. The sheer amount of space is inspiring to any artist who wishes to express themselves on a bigger scale. Their diverse members create a collaborative environment, and the exhibition space up front allows them to display works once they're complete. They hold opening and closing receptions that showcase all activity going on inside the studios.

SMITH STREET TATTOO PARLOUR
#OldSchool #SailorJerry
411 Smith Street

If you've always been jealous of your dad's sail and anchor tat, Smith Street is open and waiting to give you something that competes. Specializing in traditional design, their pieces capture the culture of American tattoos. Some of the guys here have been on the scene longer than you've been alive, but classic doesn't mean boring. Walking into this place is a little intimidating, and they don't do handholding. But if you're looking for that perfect sparrow, or something old-school with an update, the guys here will do you right.

THE ROYAL PALMS SHUFFLEBOARD CLUB
#shuffleboard #NerdGames
514 Union Street

Ever get the sudden urge to push around a puck with a broom? You're in luck. Deep down in Gowanus there's a huge industrial building that's been converted into a shuffleboard extravaganza. Never even heard of the fucking "sport"? No biggie. The concept is really easily explained over a few beers. The wait can be long, especially on league nights, where the nerdy pros take over, but once you get a court it's $40 an hour (so bring plenty of friends to split it). When you've shuffled your last board, the Royal Palms has a window where a different food truck (usually some well known Mexican vendor) pulls up and feeds you back to life. They hold a lot of corporate events here, which means you'll find a few suited tech developers or Yelp groups here on any given night.

TRIPLE DIAMOND TATTOO
#taxidermy #DentistChair
257 3rd Avenue

Nothing like a large collection of stuffed dead animals propped up postmortem to get you in the mood for a tattoo, right? Triple Diamond does not hold back on the taxidermy, cool jewelry (human molar rings!), and all kinds of oddities lining the entrance of the shop. Jon Jon is the man here, and his work is sharp and clean. When you're ready to break skin, sit back in a vintage dentist's chair and actually enjoy the pain for once. If you're looking for intricate tebori work, Takashi Matsuba (available by appointment only) is the only one in NYC who can hook you up properly.

 # SHOP

NO RELATION (L TRAIN VINTAGE)
#RealThrift #Levis
654 Sackett Street

This thrift store has many locations around Brooklyn, but the Gowanus spot is our go-to. A large, open space away from the bustle, this place smells like old wool, fur, and leather. A great place to either take your grandpa or change up your travel style to something a little more ironically old-school, the shop has all kinds of vintage T-shirts, funkadelic jackets and vests, mom jeans (and more wearable ass-coverings), printed skirts and dresses, weird Mexican shawls, crunchy hand-knit sweaters, and statement accessories. We found some super functional, barely worn, all black Chucks for $10! A fun place to experiment with fashion, this shop has all the wares to dress you like the kind of weirdo who'll blend right in with fashion-funky Brooklynites.

☺ PARTYING

BELLHOUSE
#bar #venue #DanceParty
149 7th Street

It may not be the easiest place in the world to get to, but that's kinda what makes the Bellhouse worthwhile. Walking into it feels like stepping into a classy warehouse in the '20s—which makes sense because it was a warehouse in the 1920s. There are two giant rooms, both supersexy and each with a bar serving cheap(ish) cocktails and beers. The front room is called the Frontier Room and has a stage where you can see anything from burlesque to indie rock. The other room, the Main Event Room, is gigantic—with twenty-five-foot ceilings, a huge stage, and enough space to host an elephant orgy. Given the space, you'll be able to dance without elbowing someone else in the face, even at a sold-out show. They throw a great hip-hop party called "the Rub" and often host cook-offs during the day.

GOWANUS BALLROOM
#art #party
55 9th Street

A huge, lofted warehouse space hidden along the Gowanus Canal, the Ballroom is all about large-scale art and partying to celebrate (or fundraise for) making more art. A tree house sits right in the middle of the second floor. You can climb into it and hang out with the usually strung-out weirdos who have decided to call it home for the night. They have shows that involve fire-breathers, erotica, and silk twirlers. We once went in the dead of winter and they set up an indoor lagoon. Suffice it to say, this place is weird as fuck but an excellent time if you're looking to get into something way funky. They hold parties infrequently and covers are normally under $10.

LITTLEFIELD
#LiveMusic #EventSpace
622 Degraw Street

MISSION DOLORES BAR
#bar #CheapBeer #SweatyDancing
249 4th Avenue

Littlefield holds an eclectic mix of events throughout the week. On any given day, the space can be hosting a comedy show, a famous band, a Bollywood disco, a tribute show, film screenings, art shows, sweaty dance parties fueled by nonstop reggae beats, your grandma's eightieth, or the holiday craft market. A former garage, Littlefield is now comprised of two spaces: a smaller front bar area and, if you continue through, a massive dance floor with a decent stage. Somehow, there's never really a bathroom line even when the place is filled to capacity, which is about four hundred people. An eco-conscious space, their walls are made from old tires, the bar is made up of cobbled-together bowling lanes, and the whole operation runs on wind power. The sound system here is top-notch, and whether you're getting down to some techno beats or just trying to blow up your grandma's hearing devices, Littlefield makes sure that the ringing in your ears lasts all the way until morning.

Yuenglings for $4, ample space to move around while drinking said cheap beer, and a large partially covered outdoor patio should the beers drive you to smoking. There are a few pinball machines, a bunch of other reasonably priced drafts ($4-$8), and dogs are allowed, which always serves as a good conversation starter should the dog's owner start looking mighty fine after a few. Mission Dolores always selects a wide range of music, from the pop shit that makes all the girls get squeaky, to good ol' rock and roll. Also, they don't mind if you bring in outside food, and Oaxaca across the street will deliver their delicious tacos if you're too wobbly to run through traffic on 4th Avenue.

PACIFIC STANDARD
#bar #WestCoast
82 4th Avenue

They've got a huge selection of board games, darts, and a pinball machine for active drunks and ice-cream sandwiches for lazy ones. If you hate California, keep walking, because this bar will eyefuck you with CAL banners and other questionable décor. They put on all kinds of activities, like a pub quiz on Thursdays and comedy nights. A neighborhood joint for Cali transplants and frat-house dropouts, this spot is great for having heated debates about which coast reigns. The best part is their frequent-drinkers program, a members-only club where the more spending points you rack up at the bar, the bigger the benefits (and chances of liver failure).

OTP Tip: The Standard allows you to order food for delivery and consume it on premises.

THE ROCK SHOP
#bar #LiveMusic #pool
249 4th Avenue

A two-story joint with a spacious terrace, the layout at The Rock Shop is super smart. The first floor is a huge cavern-like bar, with high ceilings, ample bar seating, and a stage at the end. They put on all kinds of performances here, from solo singer-songwriters to louder, bigger bands. The upstairs is completely isolated from the show, has its own bar, a pool table, and a bunch of TVs to watch games. The terrace is expansive with comfortable seating. If you come to The Rock Shop for a show that sucks (which doesn't really happen), you can always find ways to entertain yourself upstairs.

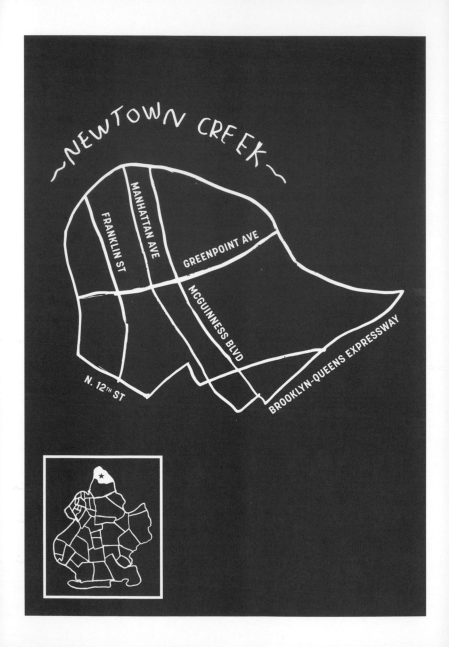

GREENPOINT

Where all the drunken Poles converge, Greenpoint is the pierogi capital of Brooklyn. With a large Polish population, walking around some parts transports you deep into a land with one too many consonants mashed together. Shop signs look like they're plucked straight from Warsaw, and old men smell of the strong drink at all hours of the day. But this place isn't all foreign; many bars and restaurants have made their way into Greenpoint via the hipster trickle from Williamsburg next door.

COFFEE AND BAKERIES

OVENLY
#bakery #PeanutButterCookies
31 Greenpoint Avenue

Ovenly is a bakery that sits right near Greenpoint's waterfront and you'll be hit with the smell of baking in progress upon entry. The shop is clean and classy up front with a big bakery in the back. The pastry case is like a glass museum, with each item given enough elbow room to be properly praised. There are muffins, scones, shorties (shortbread squares), cookies, bars, and an occasional cupcake. Each pastry is unique, with flavors that tip-toe salty and sweet set against rich, buttery backgrounds. They serve Stumptown and use the beans to make a unique shorty, with ground espresso beans incorporated throughout the buttery, not-too-sweet dough. Their peanut butter cookie is a must.

PETER PAN BAKERY
#bakery #doughnuts #CrazyCheap
727 Manhattan Avenue

These aren't Dunkin'; Peter Pan is right in the middle of Greenpoint and while they serve familiar flavors, their doughnuts (*pączki*) are done the Polish way (with the addition of a little booze to the raw batter). Your box should include: a crazy crimson-colored red velvet; a honey-dipped, glazed, chocolate cake; and a Bavarian cream-filled doughnut. They're a buck each so you can afford to splurge.

PROPELLER COFFEE
#coffee #ModDécor
984 Manhattan Avenue

The kind of place that doesn't try to be cool but embodies cool cleverness down to their website (e.g., their social media links are entitled "faces, cameras, and birds"), Propeller is accented with '60s décor, featuring black-and-white photos of stewardesses, mod lamps, and mismatched vintage chairs. Here, you'll find Elvis blaring through their speakers in the back near a nook that's perfect for catching up on e-mails. We urge you to use the bathroom (even if you don't have to) for the sole purpose of checking out the ridiculous, holographic running horse picture.

UPRIGHT COFFEE
#coffee #LavenderLatte #ToGo
860 Manhattan Avenue

A quick-fix morning joint, you run in here, grab a coffee, and get the fuck out. Called "upright" because there's really nowhere to get even partially horizontal, this shop may be small but does the job with pizzazz. They make their own almond milk and have this French lavender latte that'll subtly haunt you forever. The beans are Brooklyn Roasting Company, they've got cold brew on tap, and the pastries are from Ceci Cela (i.e., the best croissants in NYC). The train is only a few steps away, and anything you get from Upright will make your wait for the G much less grueling.

🍔 | EAT

CALEXICO
#GringoTacos #DrunkFood
645 Manhattan Avenue

What started as a taco cart by tres hermanos from California has evolved into several successful restaurants In Brooklyn. Like the town it's named after, Calexico is filled with Mexicali flavor. Start with the nachos and then try the quesadilla with crack sauce—fuck, get them to douse everything in crack sauce—it's a worthwhile addition. In this open, not heavily decorated space with a big bar and ample seating, just grabbing a taco and a jalapeño margarita should do the trick.

LOMZYNIANKA
#Polish #pierogi #BYOB
646 Manhattan Avenue

If you can't tell by all the consonants in its name, Lomzynianka is as authentic as it gets. This BYOB spot has the fluffiest, freshest pierogi in Brooklyn. To get the full experience, order the Polish platter, which is overflowing with cabbage-centric dishes, pierogies, mashed potatoes, and kielbasa. The prices are super low for generous portions of home cooking. If you're looking for dessert after your feast, the farmer's cheese pierogies or berry blintzes will add some sweetness to the carb party. The place is small, but we've never run into a problem finding a seat.

MILK AND ROSES
#chic #lunch #CountryItalian
1110 Manhattan Avenue

If you're feeling particularly gentlemanly (or ladylike), grab a light lunch (or a $22 unlimited mimosas brunch) at Milk and Roses, a Greenpoint café that looks like an Amish library. Half of the place is covered in shelves of old books, with a wooden piano right in the middle. Their lunch menu consists of Italian country-style dishes, like crispy paninis filled with cured meats and delicate cheeses. While computers do rear their ugly screens here, reading a book or having some romantic conversation feels more fitting. The waitresses are sweet, there's a just-as-nice yard for the warmer months, and because it's a ways away from the train it truly feels like a nice getaway.

PAULIE GEE'S
#FancyPizza #rustic #SpicyHoney
60 Greenpoint Avenue

The man behind the pizza spent a long time in a job he wasn't thrilled about. Then one day, he built a wood-burning oven in his yard and started tinkering with pizza. Paulie Gee's was born out of this guy's newfound passion for life, and you can taste it in every pie. The Greenpointer, a tribute pie to the neighborhood that supports his joint, is a great mingle of flavors with its crispy crust, melty cheese, and peppery, slightly wilted arugula. On the opposite spectrum, the Hellboy will convince you that spicy honey on pizza is totally a good idea. Paulie's has a super interesting menu that also includes a whole separate deal for vegans. The interior is rustic and welcoming, and the prices are fair for the quality of pie. This is a sit-down place to which you'll want to bring a group to help you devour all that pizza.

ADAM'S DELICATESSEN
#shop #food #sausages #cake
112 Nassau Avenue

Adam's is a fine Polish deli, with homemade cakes and cookies sold by the pound ($8 each) glaring at you the minute you walk in. They also do whole-fish Fridays (don't ask; just get a fish). Here, you'll find all sorts of dry goods, mustards, and jars labeled in Polish that'll hit any Eastern European immigrant with a big dose of nostalgia. The best thing here, along with their prepared salads, are their sausages. They've got a wide kielbasa collection, and this thin, hunter sausage that's smoky, gamey, and absurdly delicious. The middle-aged Polish women behind the counter, with requisite bangs, will make sure you'll never reach for a Slim Jim again.

◉ SEE AND DO

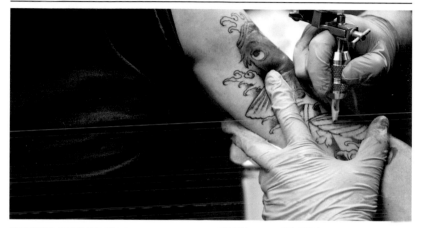

GREENPOINT TATTOO
#traditional #FreeTatAfterTenth
131 Meserole Avenue

THREE KINGS TATTOO
#birds #comfortable
492 Metropolitan Avenue

Greenpoint Tattoo does mostly traditional tattoos but is willing to work with you to get anything you want. This place is really about the vibe. If you're nervous for whatever reason, everyone here is super friendly with enough knowledge about what they're doing to ease your worries. Up there with the big guys, Greenpoint is a solid shop with a super-chill vibe. Also, if you get bitten by the tattoo bug, Chuck D. offers a free tat after your tenth.

Amid the odd mingling of hipsters and Polish drunks, you'll find Three Kings, a great little shop with incredible artists. This place isn't about pumping out boring, run-of-the-mill trendy designs. They're true artists who constantly practice the craft and come up with beautiful, twisted designs that'll rock your imagination. If you're sitting at a bar in Williamsburg and happen to notice some intricate, surrealist tattoo on the bartender's arm, chances are he got it done at Three Kings. The shop itself is your typical red-walled, lots-of-art decorated joint, but it's clean and comfortable. The tats start at $60 and increase exponentially. Not the cheapest place to get work done, but if we're talking quality and creativity, Three Kings brings it every time.

SHOP

BEACON'S CLOSET
#ThriftStore #vintage #RecentFashion
74 Guernsey Street

We have no idea who Beacon is, but his closet is full of great shit. This thrift shop focuses on maintaining a good balance of recent fashions, vintage, and costume items. Beacon's buys clothes from locals, then tags and releases them onto the racks the same day. In addition, they stock oddball novelties like fake mustaches and bow ties. You'll find that Gap sweater you haven't seen since high school but also local designer stuff that's outlived its runway fame. There is always a great selection of shoes, funky jew-elry, quirky dresses, and denim. Beacon has three closets in Brooklyn. The inventory at the Williamsburg location is quite large, so set aside a few hours to meander through their color-coded racks. If you feel like selling off the contents of your backpack, you can drop it at the buy counter, and you don't have to watch them pick through your shit while you shop.

FOX & FAWN
#ThriftStore #'80s #'90s
570 Manhattan Avenue

A midsize store that's exactly half wearable, recent vintage and half stuff only old Polish women can pull off (with a handful of H&M mixed in). The labels here are likely from '80s/'90s mail-order catalogs, with brands like Newport News and Casual Corner. You'll find some good fabrics among synthetics that'll surely give you swamp ass. They've got great worn-in leather boots and sandals, and while the glass-covered jewelry display at the counter is small, the selection is nice, with a few silver and bronze pieces to choose from. The men's section is basically a rack of color-coded vintage T-shirts. Fox & Fawn keeps their prices fair ($15-$25) so you can experiment with lots of clashing florals without going broke.

MAHPS VINTAGE
#ThriftStore #GoodQualityFabrics
#SaleRack
110 Nassau Avenue

The outdoor 50 percent-off sale rack will lure you in and is a good representation of what can be found inside. Upon entry, you'll notice how well organized everything is. Curated carefully and seasonally, Mahps doesn't bombard you with wool in the summer or booty shorts in the winter. A vintage store put together by somebody who obviously cares about aesthetics, this place is full of really great fabrics, colors, and textures. Here, you can get those chic and comfortable dresses that reveal some side-boob and are sheer enough to have a little panty peeking through. Mahps lays out rows of on-fashion shorts and pants on the middle table and is evenly split between men's and women's items. Their $20 sunglasses are great, and while you won't find big brands here, their stuff is of good quality and priced reasonably ($25-$40).

SEVEN WONDERS VINTAGE
#ThriftStore #boutique
606 Manhattan Avenue

Move past the $10 rack outside ($20 jackets), it's mostly garbage. Inside, the place is super chic for a vintage store, with carefully curated racks lining the perimeter, sparsely stocked with select pieces. You'll find some funky onesies and mumus in the mix, along with high-waisted shorts, lace, knits, a variety of prints, and awkward denim. The horse figurines and Navajo blankets on the shelves and tables give Seven Wonders a southwest feel. The men's selection is limited to one rack in the back and a handful of jewelry is displayed on a table in the middle, with several pairs of shoes and handbags strewn about. Since Seven Wonders did the digging for you, the prices are higher ($40-$60).

PARTYING

BAR MATCHLESS
#bar #wings #DayDrinking
557 Manhattan Avenue

Good for drinks and wings, this place is right near McCarren Park and they do fifty-cent wings weekdays from 3:00 to 6:00 p.m. The brunch food here is standard (huevos rancheros, biscuits and gravy, and such), and the beer selection is good and cheap. Pop in to Matchless after a game of ultimate Frisbee at the park to fuel up for round two.

BLACK RABBIT
#bar #classy #whiskey #dark
91 Greenpoint Avenue

This rabbit is pretty easy to spot, with its all-black exterior accentuated with red window panes. A little Alice in Drunkenland, a little nineteenth-century-cellar-pub chic, the Black Rabbit is impeccably designed so you can get drunk in style. They've got sexy booths, a fireplace, and a fairytale backyard. Among the usual boozy suspects, they stock some top-notch whiskey. Every table has a lamp that works double duty: A) to provide needed illumination in this dark space, and B) when you push the light on, it alerts the server of your need for another round. They don't have the system worked out seamlessly, but it's a unique feature you won't find anywhere else.

LULU'S

#bar #FreePizza #sports #LiveMusic
113 Franklin Street

Get down to the business of drinking at Lulu's, a lively two-story bar near the waterfront, with occasional live music. Not only do they have an excellent happy hour (from 3:00 to 6:00 p.m., every day), but they also give you a free cheese pizza (extra toppings are only a buck each) for every beer you buy. Sometimes you can get a beer and a shot (and a fucking pizza!) all for five bucks. Now, this isn't the kind of pizza that you get from Paulie Gee's across the street, but shit, it's decent, free, and convenient. A good place to watch a game and battle the carb lining in your stomach to the shitfaced finish line.

NO NAME BAR

#bar #dive #SecretRestaurant
597 Manhattan Avenue

No Name Bar is called such because it literally doesn't have a name, or a sign. Call this place whatever the fuck you want—if it's nice outside, or you have a craving for hole-in-the-wall Korean food, hop the G train to Nassau. The backyard is the biggest in town, and there's a "secret" Korean restaurant lurking in its spicy glory back there. Just don't get any delusions that you'll be lounging alone in the moonlight on a busy night—plan on sharing your space (and lungs) with hundreds of chain-smoking strangers.

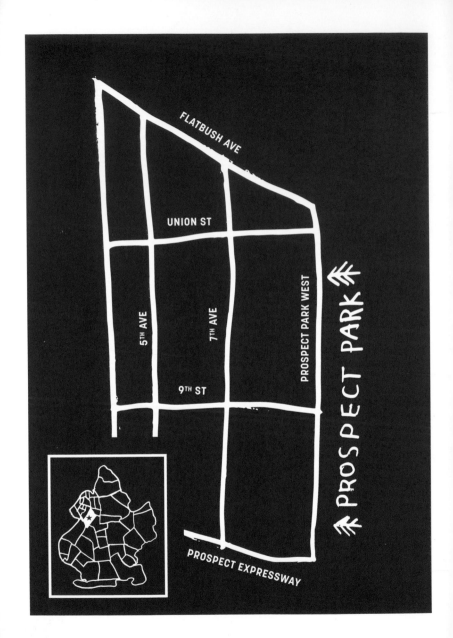

PARK SLOPE

Park Slope is the place where Brooklynites go to settle down and pop out offspring. Prospect Park is a sprawling green mass that hosts free summer music concerts (Celebrate Brooklyn), has a 3.2-mile loop with runners pounding the pavement year-round, a zoo, numerous fields, lakes, and prairies where locals gather to play with their kids and dogs. The slopes that run down from the park are lined with historic brownstones, thick greenery, and specialty shops. The two main shopping streets, 5th and 7th Avenues, house Food Network favorites like Talde, damn delicious al di la Trattoria, and Brooklyn Fish Camp. Between artisanal yogurt shops, more amazing coffee than your neurotransmitters can handle, and bars for every type of boozin', if you can get around the double strollers, Park Slope is a slanted paradise of everything your heart desires.

COFFEE AND BAKERIES

BLUE SKY MUFFINS
#bakery #muffins
53 5th Avenue

Nobody really cares about muffins, the least exciting pastry in the box. This is what we thought before we hit up Blue Sky. This place takes muffins to some level we've never seen before. Not your big-ass bodega grease ball, these muffins are smaller, lightly sweet, crunchy on the outside and moist in the inside, and come in the most interesting variety of combo flavors (like pumpkin, apple, and walnut or zucchini, raspberry, and chocolate chip). The menu changes daily, and fresh-baked muffins are brought out every hour or so. This means that any time you go, you'll likely get a warm muffin that'll suck out your soul and squeeze it until it bleeds rainbows. The shop itself is shabby-chic, with little bistro tables scattered about and speckled with ornate decorations. The owners are two of the nicest guys this neighborhood's ever seen.

CAFÉ GRUMPY
#coffee #SingleSourceBeans
#QualityBakedGoods
383 7th Avenue

A streamlined shop, this place has coffee that is known to kick you into overdrive. Their single-origin beans can get pricey per cup. If you're looking to get a little snobby, there's a list of special brews to choose your pretentious poison. Grumpy's baristas are like coffee superheros and have gone through some hardcore training to pull intense shots. Their baked goods are made at their Manhattan kitchen and are pretty

unique. Here, you'll find rose-shaped mini Bundt cakes and scones that walk the sweet/savory line with pizzazz.

CAFÉ REGULAR
#coffee #LaColombe #FeelsLikeFamily
318 11th Street

As neighborhoody as it gets, Café Regular is all about cultivating a sense of community while hitting you with the strong brew every morning. It's a tiny shop off the main 5th Avenue drag and has very few seats lining the interior, with a special window seat for those lucky enough to park there before somebody else does. The beans are La Colombe, and their iced coffee is a basement brew that's six times the strength of anything you've ever used to unhinge your eyelids. Not only is the shop super small, but there is also an awkward pole right in the middle and navigating around the place becomes a very touchy-feely-type experience. If you're feeling lost and alone in Brooklyn, Café Regular's charming baristas, cozy décor, and friendly regulars are always around to give you a big coffee hug.

FUN FACT

You've almost already been to Park Slope. *The Royal Tenenbaums, Eternal Sunshine of the Spotless Mind, Donnie Brasco,* and many *Sesame Street* episodes were all filmed here.

CULTURE: AN AMERICAN YOGURT COMPANY

#dessert #HomemadeGreekYogurt
#WetNuts

331 5th Avenue

If you thought Chobani was the epitome of Greek yogurt creaminess, Culture will prove you dead wrong. Their homemade small-batch yogurt, is so smooth that it would perfectly lube a Slip n' Slide. Culture offers at least four seasonal flavors of yogurt (like coffee caramel and coconut lime) daily. The yogurt gets pricey but the quality is top notch. They also do this thing called the Vermont Maple where they throw some "wet nuts" onto your yogurt with your choice of strawberries, banana, or blueberries. Normally wet nuts are nobody's favorite, at Culture, wet nuts are where it's at. Plus, they put a little bit of your toppings at the bottom of the cups so you're not sad about running out.

GATHER

#coffee #FoodByWeight #PicnicPerfect
341 7th Avenue

On the way to the park, your eyes will be assaulted with the hospital-teal painted all over Gather's exterior. Don't be deterred; some picnic-perfect eats lie just past the doors. While Gather is a full-service coffee shop, with in house baked goods like muffins, scones, cakes, pies, and cookies, it also offers unique, seasonal food, sold by the quarter pound. The food is healthy, fancy stuff, and while the menu rotates weekly and seasonally, they always have a big, heaping pile of kale salad and roasted chicken. The prices here stop you from pigging out, but they have specials (like a piece of chicken and two sides) that make things more affordable. Should the park be rained out, enjoy a cappuccino (made with Intelligentsia beans)

expertly crafted by well-trained baristas, with a piece of flourless chocolate cake.

GORILLA

#coffee #controversy
97 5th Avenue

Although normally known for their great Brooklyn-roasted coffee and chill neighborhood shop ambiance, this place has become better known for its behind-the-counter drama (news that made its way into the New York Times). In early April, 2010, seven nonunionized baristas straight up quit, citing mistreatment by management as their reason for dumping the place. This massive worker shortage caused Gorilla to close its doors for sixteen days and put neighborhood coffee-goers into a confused, energy-deficient frenzy. If Gorilla's closure caused this much damage, they must have been serving something worth crying about. Lucky for you, the shop is restaffed and open for business again.

WAFELS & DINGES

#dessert #StreetWaffles #Belgian
Wafel Hotline: 866-429-7329

This food truck created a waffle craze all across NYC when it first parked in SoHo in 2007. These aren't the toaster catastrophes we're all used to. These "wafels" come in two Belgian varieties—the Brussels wafel: a crispy, airy version; and the Liege wafel: a denser, chewier kind that holds up to the soggiest of dinges. It may sound like a dirty bath towel but "dinges" just means toppings. Sweet or savory, dinges include items like pulled pork, dulce de leche, Nutella, strawberries, whipped cream, walnuts, and speculoos (a buttery spread made of, goddammit, cookies). Catch the truck on weekends in Williamsburg, Carroll Gardens, and Park Slope.

WHAT THE F*CK ARE ITALIAN ICES?

Ask anybody who grew up in Brooklyn about their favorite memories of summer and we promise—between the cracked-open fire hydrants and playing makeshift baseball on the streets—there will be a place in their little hooligan hearts that remembers Italian ices.

ICE WITH AN S

Italian ices are a simple concoction of ice and a sugary flavored syrup. It's a cheap, refreshing treat during the hot New York summers that can be found all over Brooklyn, most prominently in pushcarts on the streets. But here's the thing: They're not Italian. Ices are a tangible but quickly melting symbol of Italian Americans that speaks volumes about a certain era of Brooklyn.

UNDERDOG ICE CREAM

You see, back when the second wave of Italian immigration hit, tons of southern Italians flooded Manhattan and eventually overflowed to Brooklyn. Then residents were not kind to the hordes of (what they believed to be) uneducated foreigners crowding their space. They didn't like their accents, their outfits, or their food.

So Italians banded together in communities where they found acceptance and started crafting easy, cheap foods loosely based on what they had back home. Italian ices were influenced by, but are nothing like, the granita. Ices kept Italians cool while they figured out how to fit in. Until they started making pizzas by the slice, which basically took over the New York food scene forever.

WHO THE F*CK IS GINO?

In 1955, Gino Branchinelli came to the states from Sicily and started pushing his all-natural ices, made with only ice, sugar, and puréed fruit, in little white cups. Gino was very particular about his product and kept the flavors simple and limited, with lemon being the big seller. The operation blew up, and Gino's ices made their way into dollar-slice pizza shops. Before long, "ices and slices" was the new "it thing." Nowadays, there are a bunch of places, like Louie G's, offering all kinds of variations on ices with different flavors and mix-ins.

GET YOURS

Unfortunately, Gino had a hard time keeping up with the times as he chose to keep his operation really old-school. Gino's is almost impossible to find, but for a taste of authentic ices, hit up his competitor, Louie G's (741 Union Street) in Park Slope during the summer.

Can ice really be pluralized? It's Brooklyn; just go with it.

 **EAT**

AL DI LA TRATTORIA
#dinner #ModernItalian #FamousFood
#TreatYourself
248 5th Avenue

Waiters at al di la won't brush the crumbs off your table after every bite, but the decadent food here will make you feel that fancy. If you know a thing or two about pasta, al di la will be very impressive. Always perfectly cooked and buttery but not greasy, their pasta dishes are fantastic. Go for the squid-ink spaghetti or the beet ravioli; both are beautifully presented, and while the portions are smaller than you may be used to, the flavors are rich and satisfying. Whatever you end up getting, make sure you save room for dessert. Like a rich man's doughnut, the ricotta fritters served with gooey chocolate sauce are ridiculous. Al di la's popularity means there will be a long wait most days (about an hour), and they don't take reservations. To cushion the blow, they set up a little wine bar around the corner to get you happily drunk while you wait.

BAREBURGER
#burgers #customizable
170 7th Avenue

When you're craving a big, juicy, fancy burger but don't want that tortured meat sold at most burger joints, get over to Bareburger for well-sourced, creatively topped burgers and sides. Everything here is fully customizable and the options are unique. You choose your meat, bun, three interesting veggies (we're all about the sweet apple grilled onions), bacon, cheese, and sauce (like curry ketchup or bacon marmalade). If you're lazy and just want a burger in your mouth with less options, they've thrown together some tasty topping combos (like the spicy Habanero Express or the Big Blue Bacon) and left you with the task of choosing the meat and bread. This burger joint isn't just about beef either. You can get ostrich, elk, and wild boar if you so desire. The onion rings come stacked, all of the burger creations require you to unhinge your jaw, and the staff is really friendly and open to weird requests.

BIERKRAFT
#lunch #BeerStore
#IceCreamSandwiches
191 5th Avenue

Half craft beer supermarket, half fancy sandwich shop, this is the kind of place you go when Budweiser loses its freshman cool and you're looking for something with less elephant piss and more body. On the beer side, you'll find an ever-changing selection of local craft beers in their fridges and on tap at the bar. On the sandwich side, you'll find house-made and cured meats (like pastrami-spiced brisket, paprika-rubbed wagyu roast beef, and all kinds of salami), carefully selected cheeses (manchego, cave aged gruyere, smooth and creamy Brie, and fancied-up sharp cheddar), breads, and spreads. They make all of their sandwiches to order and have specials to keep things interesting. With a beer in one hand and a sandwich in the other, head to the spacious backyard, and you've just crafted the afternoon of your dreams. Have an ice-cream sandwich (with brownies for cookies and the best gelato this side of the Atlantic) as a cherry on top of your feast.

BOGOTA LATIN BISTRO

#LatinBrunch #arepas
141 5th Avenue

Bright red and vibrant, this place screams at you from down the block, and the food here will prove that all the yellin' ain't for nothing. Working Colombian (and other Latin) food into a bistro setting, Bogota creates dishes that both stick to their Latin roots and please the palates of their Park Slope clientele. While this place is busy and dinner reservations are a must, they're great for groups, and ordering something the whole table can enjoy is easy. Get started with the empanada sampler, where you choose four of their delicious food pockets for $15 (make sure the guava one is in the mix). Move on to mains like the Colombian fritanga ($18), a combination of meats that includes chorizo, blood sausage, chicharron, and pork loin served with potatoes, tostones (plantains), and a side of aji awesome sauce. If you find yourself here for brunch, their arepa benedict ($14) will change the way you think about breakfast. Their cocktails are unique and made from fresh infusions and ingredients.

CHIPSHOP

#FriedCandyBars #UK #FamousFood
383 5th Avenue

Tourists roll into this Brit-owned joint from far and wide to partake in their one gimmick. As a publicity stunt that really stuck, Chip-Shop once advertised that it would deep-fry absolutely anything you bring in. At first, people brought in weird but edible items like Snickers bars and PB&J sandwiches. Then the Big Macs, KFC Double Downs, and sushi started making appearances in the fryer, and ChipShop hasn't been able to shake off the gimmick since. As much as the owner tries to convince people that his restaurants are more than just deep-fried garbage, nobody really gives a shit about the rest of the menu. The only thing that matters here are the fish and chips and whatever you can find in your backpack that needs deep-fry improvement.

CUBANA CAFÈ
#BrokeFancy #FlamboyantCuban
80 6th Avenue

Like the fanciest, pastel-plastered roadside Cuban shack you've ever seen, Cubana Cafè is all about hitting you with the stuff that their own cooks love to eat. Their Cuban-centric menu features classics like *ropa vieja* (old clothes . . . or torn-up, braised beef in this case), *arroz con pollo* (a Ricky Ricardo favorite), and plantains in all kinds of ways (sautèed, fried, and whipped!), plus juicy meats topped with sweet and spicy sauces and salsas. Everything is reasonably priced and the portions, while not huge, are filling. On a nice day, put on your Havana linens and grab a seat on the patio. Order something refreshing (like the ceviche or, fuck it, a mojito) and a Cuban sandwich.

DINOSAUR BBQ
#Southern #MiniChain #PorkPlate
604 Union Street

Brooklyn experienced some sort of BBQ renaissance circa 2012, and these guys are definitely at the top of that game. Save up your hunger and come here to seriously pound some Southern food. The Brooklyn outpost of several locations, Dinosaur has everything a BBQ joint should: ribs, pulled pork, brisket, shoulder, the classic sides (coleslaw, mac, BBQ beans, etc.). You can get the meat loaded onto a sandwich, a platter, or a giant combo that feeds a larger group for a good price. Dino slow-smokes everything and you can taste the process in the final product. Don't be shy, get the Big Ass Pork Plate. Their beer chandelier will remind you it's time for another round, and the beer selection will help all the animal parts jive well in their new home.

FONDA
#dinner #TreatYourself
#UpscaleMexican
434 7th Avenue

Fonda isn't some secret Mexican street cart, but Chef Antonio Santibañez does have his shit all figured out when it comes to great, nuevo-Mex flavors. Chef Santibañez has several successful restaurants in Mexico City, and while he keeps some of the menu traditional (probably to quiet the authenticity-seeker gringos), a lot of the food at Fonda is spun to spice up the classics. The tacos, taquitos (al pastor!), and enchiladas share the menu with things like guajillo burgers and braised duck zarapes. Whenever there's mole on a Mexican menu (as you'll see here), we suggest you get all over it. Fonda's is deep and luscious, made from an array of chiles and raw, stone-ground chocolate, and ladled generously over braised chicken-filled tortillas. The pork adobo, ancho-braised until it's super tender, will kick you in the mouth and make you cry.

HANCO'S
#lunch #BahnMi
350 7th Avenue

The key to great Vietnamese sandwiches is a perfect baguette. Hanco's nails the French baguette, with a crispy exterior and a warm, fluffy, stuffable interior that carries the distinct Vietnamese flavors well. While you can get a variety of fillings, the classic pork sandwich is the way to go. The meat is tender and juicy and is paired with the perfect proportion of pickled daikon, carrot, cilantro, and spicy-enough amounts of sriracha. Their 7th Avenue shop is a great pay-at-the-counter lunch spot, with enough seating and quick service.

PORK SLOPE

#brisket #FoodNetwork
247 5th Avenue

It takes balls to put the word "pork" in your restaurant name, and Dale Talde knew exactly what he was doing. As we are all aware, pork is human catnip and will draw attention and inevitably incite critique. Despite putting itself straight into the spotlight, Pork Slope has survived the discerning palates of pig eaters far and wide. You'll find a lot of classic Americana on the menu, like tater tots (which are awesome and come with any sandwich). But you don't come here for potatoes. Max out your plate with pork by ordering the pulled pork, ribs, or brisket. The more gluttonous of you(s) may be tempted to try the "mother porker," a ridiculous sandwich loaded with cheddarwurst (oh whatever, just a sausage with cheddar injected into it), bacon, a fried egg, pickled jalapeños, and griddled onions. It's good, but a little too big on pig, as the bread falls apart upon contact. Piggyback a few whiskey shots and if your pants haven't yet exploded, head over to the pool table in the back and grease up the cues with your porky hands.

SONG

#lunch #dinner #BrokeFancy #Thai
295 5th Avenue

A super-affordable, yet extra fancy-looking joint on the foodie stretch of Park Slope, Song's papaya salad (Som Tum) is the best we've had (and it's under $4!). Sure, every Thai restaurant has one of these on the menu, but something about Song's is spot-on. It's both sweet and sour, a little spicy, and the vegetables are all fresh and perfectly julienned. Their ability to strike a balance using traditional Thai flavors doesn't just stop at salad. Song's spicy noodles, with a chili basil sauce, are amazing and the massaman curry is rich and flavorful like it should be. The interior is a wide open space, and if you wanted to bring a huge group, they'd be able to seat and feed all of you for less than the price of a couple large pizzas.

TALDE

#dinner #FoodNetwork
369 7th Avenue

Locals either love this place or are completely, extremely over it because of the massive hype it received upon opening. Its owner is Dale Talde of *Top Chef* fame, and while he owns other neighborhood restaurants, this eponymous joint seems the closest to his foodie heart. The pork-heavy menu is Asian-inspired, with cheffy versions of ramen, pad thai, short ribs, and thom ka (lobster). Since Dale was raised Filipino, the dessert here (and the only one he knows how to make, according to *Top Chef*) is little-known "halo-halo," a traditional dish that throws all kinds of things over shaved ice and condensed milk; Dale's version includes some fairly common ingredients, like tapioca and pineapple, with a handful of Cap'n Crunch to keep it interesting. While some items aren't really worth it (eh on the ramen), the pretzel pork and chive dumplings are amazing and deserve the hype. With fame comes a long wait, but once you get inside, the restaurant's dark wood booths are comfortable and the open kitchen is fun to watch.

 SEE AND DO

BARCLAY'S CENTER
#BigNameShows #BrooklynNets
#Beyoncé
620 Atlantic Avenue

Opened in 2012, the Barclay's Center looks like a massive spaceship that crash-landed in Park Slope. While the residents were skeptical of its arrival at first, they have learned to embrace the massive crowds that trample down Atlantic Avenue whenever big acts come to town. This multi-faceted arena serves as a stadium for the Brooklyn Nets, a skating rink for Disney on Ice, a venue for the MTV Video Music Awards show, a stage for all kinds of performers like Billy Joel and the Red Hot Chili Peppers, and as the covered backyard of Jay-Z and Queen B, who regularly pop in to sing a few songs for money. At Barclay's, the regular stadium concessions get the Brooklyn treatment, with Nathan's Famous hot dogs, L&B Spumoni Gardens' Sicilian slices, Fatty 'Cue's mouthwatering BBQ, Mexican food favorite Calexico, and cheesecake God Junior's all peddling their delicious goods inside. Barclay's holds bigger events and ticket prices range accordingly. It's not huge, so the nosebleeds will still be a good view.

BROOKLYN BOULDERS
#RockClimbing #Bouldering
575 Degraw Street

These guys have dedicated 18,000 square feet to nothing but climb. Like a tricked-out skate park, Boulders has neon rocks jammed into every elevated crevice of their expansive outdoor space. If you like hanging on for dear life upside-down, this is definitely the place for you. For $30 (or $24 for students), you get a day pass and a quick orientation to learn the rocky ropes and it's $11 to rent all the gear (shoes, harness, and chalk bag) you need to get you up that wall.

GREEN-WOOD CEMETERY
#scenic #historic
500 25th Street

A massive cemetery that lies a little outside of Park Slope and seems to stretch forever when viewed from the train, Green-Wood is the final resting place for famous Civil War generals, American pioneers in various fields, baseball legends, and Jean-Michel Basquiat. Almost 200 years old and stretched across 478 acres, Green-Wood has some impressive places to chill among the dead. You can kick back surrounded by old trees and watch some interesting birds fly by. The tombstones and mausoleums here are cool and beautifully falling apart. Green-Wood is pretty far from all the action of the rest of Brooklyn and a quiet place to go get your morbid on.

HAND OF GLORY TATTOO STUDIO
#clean #skilled
429 7th Avenue

You'd think mommy-and-me Park Slope wouldn't be much of a tattoo neighborhood, but Hand of Glory breaks through that baby skin and deposits some fresh ink. Great for first-timers, the talented artists here will work with you until you're completely satisfied. Now, this doesn't mean they'll let you cry in their laps until you stop being a sissy, but if you've got an idea for what you want but don't quite possess the skills to visually express it, Hand of Glory will produce some awesome sketches to help bring it to life. They're reasonably priced for the quality and work very fast. The End Is Near, their sister shop down the street, is fantastic for piercings. Anything we've ever gotten there healed faster than rug burn.

LEATHERNECKS TATTOO
#DanBones #GoodEquipment
667A 5th Avenue

You might be a little intimidated walking in, but worry not, there are plenty of pictures of well-shaped bosoms hanging on the walls to dissipate any of your fears (or at least distract you while you're getting poked). Whispers about the top quality of Dan Bones's work can be heard far and wide. He's the dude you see if you're going for something intricate with fine, straight lines. Their prices are average, they all work quickly, and their equipment is top-notch.

PRIDE PARADE
#ColorfulGays
500 25th Street

The Brooklyn version of a national parade that happens during gay pride week each summer, this festival revolves around acceptance, love, and awareness. A big ol' gay party, the Pride Parade has been an exciting event for Brooklyn's large LGBT community for two decades. You don't have to be gay to play; slap on some rainbow gear and get tangled in the crowds of happy people celebrating their right to love whomever they want.

PROSPECT PARK
#bike #run #picnic #LiveMusic
429 7th Avenue

Built by Central Park's architects, Frederick Law Olmsted and Calvert Vaux, Prospect Park is a massive green giant that connects a wide array of Brooklyn neighborhoods. Spread across sixty-five acres, the park is full of big open fields and prairies, a huge lake that's perfectly serene in the morning, winding pathways, BBQ areas, a doggie pond, an outdoor gym, a zoo, and a summer stage built for Celebrate Brooklyn's (mostly free) concerts put on by BAM. Year-round, you'll find people jogging and biking along the 3.2-mile scenic loop that surrounds the park. Come here for picnics, to play some Frisbee, to tan topless, catch a concert, or make out in some remote corner. It may not be as famous as Central Park, but that only means there's a lot more breathing room (and secluded areas for, ahem, heaving breathing).

COLOR RUN

It's a great scene when you're just walking around, minding your business, and a group of sweaty, brightly colored people surround you wearing sneakers and spandex. Started in 2012, the Color Run is an untimed and unjudged 5K run that's all about health, happiness, and personal achievement. For every kilo you complete, you get rewarded by being doused in colorful powder, which results in a messy rainbow at the finish line. Inspired by India's Holi festival, paint parades, and mud runs, the Color Run has become an international event held in more than 130 destinations worldwide each year. Brooklyn's version starts at Floyd Bennett Field and many runners end up in Park Slope, spreading joy and color dust all over the streets for the after-party.

🏪 **SHOP**

BABELAND
#SexShop #classes
462 Bergen Street

A sex shop that's not as seedy as most, Babeland is all about keeping an open mind about sex and the toys that make it fun. They sell everything from vibrators to anal beads, lubes to jerk tubes, oils, condoms, strap-ons, and just about anything you can imagine. They're huge on sex education and hold fun lectures, seminars, and in-store demonstrations. They also encourage you to "come for a cause" by regularly contributing to charitable organizations that further AIDS awareness, help with positive sex education, and support equal rights for the LGBT community. A great place to work out your kinks, Babeland is a progressive store with a lot of fun and sexy merchandise.

BEACON'S CLOSET
#ThriftStore #'80s #'90s
92 5th Avenue

The Park Slope outpost of a mini-chain thrift shop, this Beacon's Closet is smaller than the rest and stocked with clothes you were too young to wear when your mom was rocking them. They have a lot of mid-'90s florals, dresses, and boots. Here, you'll find gently worn brands from the recent past like the Limited and Calvin Klein. The men's section is quite tiny but has a good selection of button-downs and jeans. They also carry a lot of unique accessories, some new and others pulled straight from your mom's jewelry junk box. You can also sell your stuff at the buy counter in the back to make some extra pocket change for your shopping spree.

BROOKLYN SUPERHERO SUPPLY CO.
#GimickyStore #capes #WindTunnel
372 5th Avenue

Listen, capes and spandex onesies don't just appear out of thin air. Where Batman goes for belt buckles, and where the Hulk gets his greens, the Brooklyn Superhero Supply store is perhaps the most ridiculous shop in these strange parts. Park Slope locals are incredibly confused about the purpose of this store, and we won't lie, it's generally a very confusing place. You can buy a secret identity kit, a vapor blaster, and a gallon of gravity in a jar for $14. You can get a cape here and try it on in a wind tunnel! Really, if we told you any more, everything would be ruined. Except that all this foolery is for a good cause—one that you'll find behind a trapdoor in the store.

HOUSING WORKS THRIFT SHOP
#ThriftShop #clothes #furniture
#GoodCause
266 5th Avenue

If you want to secondhand shop for a cause, Housing Works is an organization whose mission is to help alleviate AIDS and home-lessness through interesting entrepreneur-ial businesses, like thrift shops. Here, you'll not only find clothes and accessories but also furniture, housewares, and all kinds of other knickknacks. Donated by people who care, some of the stuff here is pretty nice, and while it's a little pricier than other thrift shops, you can find real silver jewelry and some serious brands, all while contributing to the greater good of the community. It's kind of a hit or miss, and the selection isn't very large, but popping in for a few minutes to check out the wares is never a bad idea.

SUMMER STOOP SALES
#StreetShopping
Stoops all over Park Slope

Nobody does a stoop sale like Park Slope because the neighborhood has more stoops per square inch than anywhere else. During the summer (and come spring), stoops all over Park Slope are littered with random items. You can hit just about any block on a Saturday and trade your $10 for an eclectic collection of incense holders, worn-in boots, and a special edition *Star Wars* Monopoly. Plus, around 5:00 p.m., when it's time to set-tle in for dinner, the unsold goods of the day get thrown up on the surrounding fences and are free for the taking.

PARTYING

BARBES
#bar #LiveMusic #SlavicSoulParty
376 9th Street

This bar is great for live music any night. Made up of two areas, one for drinking and the other for music, the front is great for putting on your dancing shoes via liquid courage. The back room is soundproofed, with a door separating it from the main space, but a system is set up that feeds the front bar with the music playing live in the back at a reasonable, balanced volume. All this organized music listening gets thrown out the door on Tuesdays during the Slavic Soul Party, when the Eastern European jams take over the whole place and you will be left with no choice but to dance like crazy. A little gypsy, a little punk, Barbes brings the beats hard, and while you may mangle a few toes, this place will shake up your Soviet loving soul.

DOUBLE WINDSOR
#bar #LaidBack
210 Prospect Park West

Despite the name, the only thing you'll be tying on in this bar and restaurant is a solid buzz. The biggest standout about Double Windsor is how little it stands out—this is the perfect spot to grab a beer, eat some sriracha wings, and just chill. The typical bar food is better-than-normal, and the beer selection is solid. Cash is king here, so be sure and have some on hand.

FREDDY'S BAR
#bar #eclectic #ComedyShow
627 5th Avenue

Eclectic is definitely the word for this place, but let's see if we can paint a clearer picture. You know when your aunt buys some hideous thing at a garage sale for a quarter (like a lamb's head mounted on a walking stick with the words "Mary had a little limp" on it) and claims that it's a conversation piece? Well, Freddy's is plastered with "conversation pieces." The lighting is weird and dark, and there's a video monitor that plays some twisted shit in the window. It may sound nutty (and it is), but Freddy's is always a good time. They host a free comedy show in their back room every Monday, allowing local comedians to practice their new material on drunk guinea pigs before performing for the big shots at other venues.

HIGH DIVE
#bar #NotaDive #FreePopcorn
243 5th Avenue

Painted a bold red, this place is easy to locate even if you've already put in some pre-pregaming time elsewhere. A true-to-the-name oxymoronic high-end dive, there's nothing sleazy about the joint. They always have a great selection of beers on tap, from requisite PBRs to our favorite, light and crisp Allagash White. There's a self-serve popcorn machine, with all kinds of spices you can shake on (Old Bay!). The atmosphere here is right for shooting the shit. If plain conversation gets lame, they've got board games, a pinball machine, and a bathroom with chalk walls so you can use one hand for relief and the other for self expression. Wash both.

SEA WITCH
#bar #FishTank #nautical #backyard
703 5th Avenue

The kind of bar that'll impress potential lays, Sea Witch has a nautical theme running throughout, but not in the cheesy, peg legs and parrots sort of way. The entrance is a boat front, and the food window is the first thing you see as you walk in. Circle back to the amazing bar food once you've had a chance to poke around. The bar itself is long and sweeping, with an incredible oval fish tank that glows a soothing blue, filled with tropical fish that rhythmically swim to the well-picked tunes. Don't get stuck fish-watching too long; there's an insane backyard to explore. Past the underwater witchy mural and through the double doors in the back, the yard is arranged with lounging in mind, with cascading rocks, pebbled walkways, a flowing koi pond, and ample seating. When you finally settle down in the Sea, order up some fried oysters, maybe a fish taco or two, and a Jack Rose, a citrusy cocktail with Laird's apple brandy that'll help the seafood swim down with ease. If conversation ever comes to a standstill, the fish tank is always around to keep your eyes busy.

Union Hall

SKYLARK

#bar #FreeCandy #ShotSpecials

477 5th Avenue

This bar is all in the details. The menu is filled with awkward family photos, the kind where your uncle is reclining on an old chair with a whiskey in hand. There are bowls of hard candy laid out randomly around the place, with peppermints, butterscotch, and all the other reject Halloween candy that nobody likes in their pumpkin pails. The beer and shot specials are always good, and their bar food is classy. Take the party to the white-picket-fenced seating area around the corner and watch South Slope roll by.

UNION HALL

#bar #bocce #LiveMusic #MeatMarket

702 Union Street

Park Slope's version of a hook-up meat market, Union Hall usually draws a young crowd. Built inside a converted warehouse, Union Hall is jammed with all kinds of different spaces so you can feel like you're bar-hopping without ever having to go outside (except if you want to hit the garden out on the side for a cig). When you walk in, the front is built like a library, with stacks of books, comfy grandpa armchairs, a fireplace, and a twirly world globe. The back area will be hard to decipher at first, but back there lie two bocce ball courts, a game of skillfully throwing balls down a long stretch. There are "pro" leagues here so bring your A game. The downstairs is an event space, and they host all kinds of performances, from no-name bands to random international stars to bands like the Ting Tings. Sometimes they'll do comedy, weird performances, and DJed dance parties.

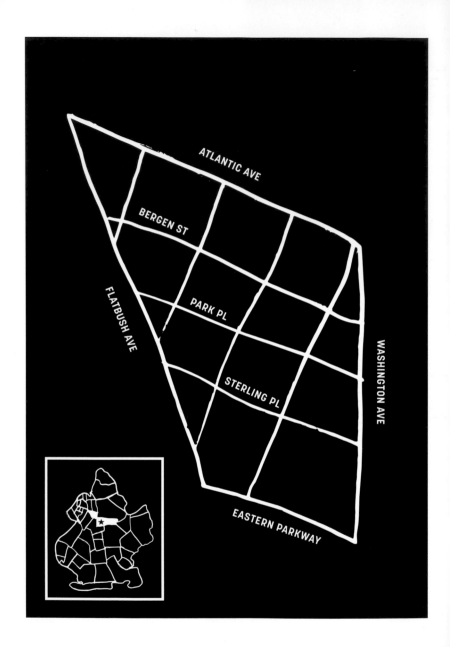

ATLANTIC AVE

BERGEN ST

FLATBUSH AVE

PARK PL

STERLING PL

WASHINGTON AVE

EASTERN PARKWAY

PROSPECT HEIGHTS/ CROWN HEIGHTS

Formerly a neighborhood populated by mostly Hasidic Jews, Crown Heights has joined (then mostly West Indian) Prospect Heights as the new "it" neighborhood. Their borders are blurred, and many (super-uncool) people refer to the conglomerate as "ProCro." In the Pro part, you'll find a lot of trendy midprice restaurants, gastropubs, and prewar buildings, built tall to tower over nearby Prospect Park, Brooklyn Museum, Brooklyn Public Library, and Grand Army Plaza, where a bustling farmers' market goes down every Saturday. The Cro part runs along Eastern Parkway and has an interesting blend of residents, many of West Indian and Hasidic descent. We can't say they live together in seamless, handholding harmony, but it does create a unique demographic that celebrates their own respective cultures, sometimes simultaneously.

COFFEE AND BAKERIES

AMPLE HILLS CREAMERY
#FancyIceCream #CrackCaramel
623 Vanderbilt Avenue

Brian Smith, a former science fiction writer, thinks Brooklyn is the fairytale town. The shop is named after a line in Walt Whitman's "Crossing Brooklyn Ferry." Smith first pushed his magical ice cream to concertgoers in Prospect Park before setting up a for reals shop on foodie-famous Vanderbilt nearby. The base of his ice cream is just eggs, milk, and sugar, all from local, upstate New York farms, and if you're not feeling very adventurous, the plain vanilla shines on its own. For something truly extraordinary though, test drive the salted crack caramel, a deep orange–hued, salted butter caramel base with little chunks of crack cookies stirred in. Their menu somewhat changes and the flavors are outrageous but super good, with cake chunks, cookies, fudge, pretzels, and honeycomb candy finding their way into your cone (which has a swirly, whirly pattern for added fairy flair).

OTP Tip: Their newest location in Gowanus (305 Nevins Street) is a massive two-story ice-cream funhouse with a roof deck. It's the only location that serves the "It Came from Gowanus" flavor, which is a messy mix of chocolate and maybe gonorrhea.

FUN FACT
Walt Whitman was fired from the *Brooklyn Daily Eagle* in 1848.

HUNGRY GHOST
#coffee #pastries #kombuchas
253 Flatbush Avenue

Classier than most coffee joints, Hungry Ghost is not the old, worn-down armchair type. They get a lot of shit for not allowing computers at their best tables up front, but there's a bar section dedicated to laptop farms that wraps around the middle. In addition to stellar coffee, this joint dispenses kombucha on tap (you know, that fizzy healthy drink that comes from moldy mushrooms?). The place is big and the lighting is dim enough so you can drink your hippie drinks out in the open with pride.

SIT AND WONDER
#coffee #CoolDécor
688 Washington Avenue

A little dusty with a lot of charm, Sit and Wonder is a good neighborhood shop in a part of town that doesn't have the high concentration of fancy coffee normally found in north Brooklyn. Old books line the front platform of the shop, with barstools positioned to watch the foot traffic outside through the front window. The baristas here are completely unjaded by the whole coffee snob culture and serve up their Stumptown with zero pretension. Get any of their shots expertly blended with homemade almond milk for something surprisingly delightful. Their to-stay mugs depict grazing cows, the pastries are half off after 5:00 p.m., and with all that good atmosphere, you too will be tempted to make a lame joke about sitting and wondering.

EAT

BARK HOT DOGS
#AustrianDogs #BrokeFancyToppings
474 Bergen Street

Everyone has messed with the hot dog in some way, and the guy at Bark saw a lot of opportunity when presented with the blank dog, bun, and sauce canvas. At Bark, chef Josh Sharkey takes the humblest of "casual" food and transforms it into something fancier by sourcing prime ingredients (like his Austrian-style hot dogs that he painstakingly perfected for five years), treating them like fast food and more like real food, all the while sticking to the nostalgic, Americana feel of the good 'ol dog. The origin of every single item is listed on their site and in-store, which keeps things at Bark real honest. There are chili dogs, mustard-and-onion dogs, and a cheesy bacon-cheddar dog. The heirloom baked beans, slow-cooked for several hours with bacon and ham hock, are absolutely amazing and can be thrown on top of a dog at your request.

BORN THAI
#ModernThai #VegFriendly
#CoconutWater
293 Flatbush Avenue

A modern Thai joint that lays out their menu in a DVD cover, all separated by ingredients like meat, fish, and vegetables. Born is easy for when you're in a group with varied dietary needs; they are focused on pleasing all kinds of eaters with their dishes. The interior, with its clean tables, classy centerpiece bar, mood lighting, and decorative wall plates, makes you feel fancy while the prices keep things real. They've also got a white-Christmas-light-illuminated yard for dining when the weather's right. The food itself is a little different than your typical Thai joint. They've got all the classics on the menu, like cop-out eater favorite pad thai, but the dishes are reimagined with tamarind sauces, dramatic presentations (check out the whole fried fish), and al dente fresh vegetables. A weird favorite of ours is their coconut water, which comes with chunks of coconut meat to give it a little something extra.

CHAVELA'S
#dinner #Mexican #brunch
736 Franklin Avenue

Chavela's is overflowing with freshness and practically gives away their amazing tacos during happy hour (4:00 to 7:00 p.m. during the week) for $2 each. Not interested in tacos with a few dainty pieces of meat and lettuce thrown into a tortilla, Chavela's stuffs that thing with heaps of tender beef, chicken, or fish, and douses it with the right proportion of sauce and toppings. If you're looking to go big, get a Plato Don (your choice of veggie, meat, or fish), a DIY food coma with rice, beans, guac, queso, fresh salsa, and tortillas. They do brunch right for $11.95; every platter is overflowing with eggs, beans, sauces, and salsas. The décor here is rustic and the full-of-fruit sangrias ($5 during happy hour) will blow you away.

CHUKO

#ramen #winter
552 Vanderbilt Avenue

If the New York winter unexpectedly kicks you in the ass, pop into Chuko for a steaming bowl of ramen. Ramen aficionados will tell you that good ramen is all about the broth, and Chuko has it nailed. From their popular vegetarian ramen (which is hard to do because the flavor is normally coaxed from pork or fish), to their deeply flavorful kimchi ramen (made with pork), this place knows how to throw together a comforting bowl of Asian soup. The inside is a glowing red beacon of warmth, and the soup will get you all cozy and ready to deal with the treachery outside.

OTP Tip: Don't want to pay $13 for ramen? Hop across the street to Bar Chuko, their izakaya, for some cheaper options like chicken gizzard skewers ($2.50).

KAZ AN NOU

#FancyCaribbean #JerkChicken #BYOB
53 6th Avenue

Before we even delve into their delicious Caribbean-French food, we need you to know this place is BYOB with no corking fee. That means you can bring a six-pack and not pay the usual 200 percent markup on beer. Now, let's focus. Jerk chicken! This place smokes and rubs their bird down with those

good spices and serves it with a creamy goat cheese, tarragon, and honey sauce. It looks a little messy when it gets to you, but it is damn delicious going down. The service is a little slow, but sitting around with your own bottle of booze will pass the time well.

PETEZAAZ

#wacky #PotatoPizza
766 Classon Avenue

Talk about reinventing the pizza wheel! PeteZaaz isn't your mama's pizzeria, and we wouldn't have it any other way. We have dreams about the baked potato pizza, served up with crème fraîche, white cheddar, smoked bacon, and Andean purple potatoes. The split pea and chicken fried steak pizzas are totally worth writing home about too. They have other stuff on the menu, but PeteZaaz should be able to make pizza your thing if it's not already. The dine-in area is pretty small though; weather permitting, we recommend grabbing a pizza to go and eating in nearby Prospect Park.

TOM'S

#diner #legend
782 Washington Avenue

A classic Brooklyn diner with a cult following, Tom's will feed you till you bleed. Around since 1936, Tom's menu includes everything you'd expect. Hearty breakfast dishes piled high with eggs and bacon and the best damn lemon ricotta pancakes we've ever had. Everything is made fresh, served with butter and all the fixin's, and will never cost more than breakfast should. It's an older Brooklyn fixture that has managed to evolve just enough to please new palates while maintaining its charm.

◉ SEE AND DO

BROOKLYN BOTANIC GARDEN
#flowers #trees #exhibits
150 Eastern Parkway

A hundred-plus-year-old massive botanical garden that buzzes with activity year-round, the area is split up into various gardens (some with roses, some with exotic plants), fields (like the all-purple lavender field, or an open grassy area covered in cherry blossom trees), architectural structures (like a lake with a giant pagoda), and greenhouse-covered tropical plants. Come here with clear sinuses because everything smells incredible. It's big enough to hold your interest but won't kill your legs as it can be circumvented in a few hours. While for obvious reasons spring is the best time to go, the Botanical Garden provides incentives (like their heated indoor exhibits) to draw in wintertime visitors. Admission to the garden is free on Tuesdays, Saturdays from ten to noon, and winter weekdays.

BROOKLYN MUSEUM
#InternationalArtExhibits #lectures
#FirstSaturdayParty
200 Eastern Parkway

When you walk up the wrapping staircase that leads to the entrance of the Brooklyn Museum, you'll feel like some sort of royalty. The museum is one of the oldest in the country, and its permanent collection consists of cool artifacts from various cultures, some of which date back to ancient Egypt. These parts of the museum will take a full day to navigate if you're the reading and learning type; the sculpture garden is a good place to give your brain a rest. The Brooklyn Museum keeps the arts alive by putting together exhibits that display the works of a wide variety of current international artists from every genre including fashion, film, and large-scale works. Also, every first Saturday of the month, Target throws a big ol' free party from 5:00 to 11:00 p.m. that adds a little music and entertainment to the museum mix.

OTP Tip: If you want to support the arts but can only afford to throw a buck their way, you can still enter. The signs indicating admission look very tricky. The suggested donation for adults is $12 and $8 for students, but they only tell you about the "suggestion" part of it via an asterisk and small print.

HOW TO DO VANDERBILT ON THE CHEAP

Vanderbilt Street has gained its gold stars with food enthusiasts in recent years. The Vanderbilt (570 Vanderbilt Avenue) is the most popular joint on the block, and its fancy $12 pork sausages and $11 cocktails will set you back a pretty penny. Navigating the (still cheaper than Manhattan) bank-breaking gastropubs can be tricky. Here are a few spots on Vanderbilt that'll let you stroll around full, drunk, and financially secure.

THE USUAL

If your perfect Saturday morning still consists of cartoons and pancakes, The Usual (637 Vanderbilt Avenue) will feed your childish desires for about five bucks. Big daddy breakfast platters, with eggs, grits, home fries, toast, and meaty add-ons are never more than eight bucks. Sit down, order a coffee for a $1.50, and proceed to load breakfast into your face until you're ready to roll.

STROLL, IT'S FREE

Vanderbilt is really beautiful, and ain't nobody charging you to walk around. Take some photos of the shops and tree-lined streets.

WOODWORK

If a game of any sort is on the tube, Woodwork (583 Vanderbilt Avenue) is a good place to be. The $15 Fuckitbucket (six cheap beers for the price of five) is not the most incredible deal on PBRs and Bud Lights, but it'll secure you a lively place to watch whatever sport you're into. Their happy hour, where drafts and well drinks are only $4, runs from 4:00 to 7:00 p.m.

SODA BAR

Soda Bar (629 Vanderbilt Avenue) is a grungy dive with a long and strong happy hour. A lucky seven hours of drinking, the noon to 7:00 p.m. (weekdays) happy hour knocks beers down to $3 and well drinks to $5. Nobody will get mad at you for breaking out the dance moves; there's a nice patio and the weekends sometimes turn into a shit show in the back room.

606 R&D

When the fuck is supper? We like to think of it as the night equivalent of brunch, and 606 R&D (606 Vanderbilt Avenue) does a good take on this mixed-up meal for $25 per person. The regular menu here is way up there pricewise, but on Sundays this little splurge will get you a whole bunch of food, served family style. The menu changes weekly but is always hearty and includes an app, a main (with several sides), and dessert.

BROOKLYN PUBLIC LIBRARY (CENTRAL)

#books #FreeConcerts
10 Grand Army Plaza

OK, so this is a library with books in it, big deal. But it seems to draw the tourist crowds just like every other big attraction in the area. Maybe it's because the building is shaped like an open book, and has a fifty-foot door? Or the free concerts and WiFi in the plaza? Whatever the draw, this house of books has had more facelifts than Madonna and continues to thrive during the digital era.

GRAND ARMY PLAZA

#monument #FarmersMarket
Northern corner of Prospect Park

A semicircular plaza at the north entrance of Prospect Park most noted for containing the historical Sailors' and Soldiers' Triumphal Arch, a monument dedicated to those who fought for the Union during the Civil War. The plaza itself was really built as a separator from the busy street and the serene park. Made up of a bunch of ovals and only foot traffic, the plaza explodes with activity on Saturdays when the farmers' market rolls in with fresh local food, awesome cooking demonstrations, and local musicians (and sometimes a creepy clown). The best way to do the plaza is by taking a Saturday-morning jog along the park loop counter-clockwise from the south end and ending your run at the plaza with a few fresh market apples (or pie).

WEST INDIAN AMERICAN DAY CARNIVAL

#carnival #performances

A Caribbean pride and culture festival, this event gets ridiculously wild every year on Labor Day. People go all out with Carnival costumes, booty-bumpin' music, island food, and elaborate floats. Deemed "the Greatest Show on Earth," the festival celebrates both the individual West Indian cultures and their combined heritage. Steel-drum bands, youth performance competitions, salsa, calypso, reggae, and soca make for a loud party that draws millions of spectators each year to the Grand Army Plaza and along the parade's Eastern Parkway procession route.

SHOP

BKLYN LARDER
#SpecialtyFood #meat #cheese
#sandwiches
228 Flatbush Avenue

BKLYN Larder is a superstore of specialty foods. From jams to meats, cheese to chocolate, these guys picked through the abundance of Brooklyn's artisanal super scene (and other small batch businesses around the world) and hoarded it all in their store. The high prices are reflective of the quality of their items, and while it might feel a little froufrou, everything here is mad tasty. Trust us, you won't be able to just run in here, buy a jar of jam, and be out because their prepared foods will detain you for some time. They've got all kinds of sides and salads, roasted chicken, pasta dishes, delicate fish, meatballs, and fresh-baked pastries of the sweet and savory varieties (apple bacon scones, bitches!). You cannot leave here without gelato. The hole in your wallet will be of equal proportion to the joy in your heart.

PARTYING

FRANKLIN PARK
#bar #SweatyDancing #HipHop
618 Saint Johns Place

If a sweaty, carefree dance party is what you're after, Franklin Park brings it hard every time. Away from the Williamsburg crowd, this bar has a happening yard and an always-packed interior bar space, and it is attached to a burger joint should you need a calorie boost after shaking it for so long. The music here isn't your Katy Perry, Gaga bullshit. Sometimes it's underground hip-hop from way back (or some current stuff), non-Skrillex electronica, a bit of reggae, and sometimes all of the above in one night. Despite the madness, the bartenders always know when you're waiting for a drink and won't give you dirty looks if you just need some water.

WEATHER UP
#bar #Speakeasy
589 Vanderbilt Street

You can identify unmarked Weather Up by walking up trendy Vanderbilt until you see something that looks like a white-tiled subway station emitting an amber glow. Come here for old-school cocktails, particularly the old-fashioned (which comes with little cubes of ginger). The whole place, with its white tiles extending up over the ceiling and big, box lighting, will make you feel like you're waiting for the subway (but luckily, you're just waiting for a delicious drink). Slip into one of their booths and do whatever's clever under the cover of darkness.

THE WAY STATION
#bar #nerds #DrWho
683 Washington Avenue

This one is for the big nerds out there. The Way Station is a *Doctor Who*-themed bar and is super dedicated to fulfilling all your nerdy, sci-fi-loving needs. All the drinks are named after someone or something on the show, the place is decked out in relevant memorabilia, and the big nerd draw is the TARDIS bathroom. The performances are all dork-centric with regular *Doctor Who* screenings, nerd karaoke, cabaret, and other super-geeky events. Their happy hour runs every day, and your $4 beer is pulled out of a steampunk tap. Come here to live in pretend-British TV land for a night.

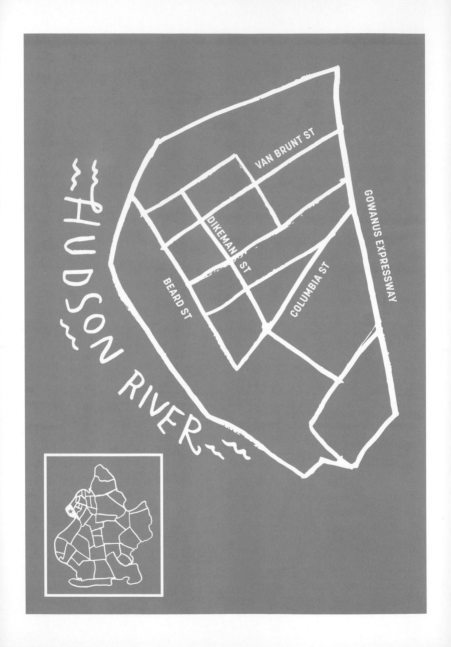

RED HOOK

Although the sorest thumb in Red Hook is the big IKEA sticking out on the port, there is much more to this hood than particle-board and frozen meatballs. A close-knit community along the East River, back in 2012, Red Hook was badly hit by Hurricane Sandy. People were trapped in their homes with no electricity, businesses were flooded for weeks, and garbage was floating around in a postapocalyptic mess. In a true display of the Brooklyn spirit, residents banded together to rebuild their community after the storm, and the result is something extraordinary. While some damaged bits remain, the people of Red Hook are that much more united, and you can feel the homey, neighborly love at every bar and restaurant. Semi-industrial port, semi-cozy Brooklyn home-livin', Red Hook is all about lobster, craft beers, and lazy waterfront afternoons.

COFFEE AND BAKERIES

BAKED

#bakery #coffee #FamousFood
#brookster
359 Van Brunt Street

The idea behind Baked is to take the simple treats from your childhood and give them wings. You like cookies? How about brownies? Well, they smush the two together to create a "Brookster," something your mom would never let you eat in one sitting. The owners are all about digging through the annals of Americana, pulling out recipes that need some remixing, and baking up newfangled treats without holding back on the good stuff. They've got Girl Scout Samoas all figured out with their caramel-coconut cluster bars, classic mallow cups are redone with their made-from-scratch fluffy marshmallows, and giant whoopie pies get stuffed full of buttercream in seasonal varieties. The shop is long and wooden, with an exposed baking area and a counter cluttered with the goods that have earned Baked its Food Network notoriety.

STEVE'S AUTHENTIC KEY LIME PIES

#dessert #KeyLimePie #SteveIsNuts
185 Van Dyke Street

Yeah, you'd think this place just has a kooky name but makes a bunch of other things like apple pie, or cookies or something. Nope. Key lime pie. Nothing else. Steve's philosophy is that all these new-age bakeries are trying too hard to diversify their menus with tarts covered in bacon candy and all that other bullshit. Steve feels key lime pie has been pushed into a corner and that he's responsible for rescuing that poor pie. Steve's like your weird uncle who keeps giving you Slinkies for Christmas, and his website is far beyond ridiculous. But that man really knows his key lime pies. To find the shop, you'll have to follow some handwritten, neon-colored signs until you feel like you're getting lured into a rape den. If the roll-up gate is open (which happens pretty sporadically; warm weekends from 11:00 a.m. to 6:00 p.m. are your best bet), you will be rewarded with fresh key lime pie (available in four sizes, including the chocolate-dipped "swingle"), and a weird sense that you're back in the '90s.

 # EAT

DEFONTES

#lunch #FattySandwiches
379 Columbia Street

An old-school sandwich shop started by someone's Italian grandad. They're not panini Italians; they're "hero" Italians. Everything here is fresh and comes on a big-ass loaf of bread. The potato and egg is a classic that never disappoints, but their pastrami, steak pizzaiola, and eggplant varieties are killer. Every sandwich is stuffed to the bready brim. You'll need to choose between a small (fucking huge) and a large (hibernation inducing).

RED HOOK LOBSTER POUND

#LobsterRolls #TreatYourself
284 Van Brunt Street

Red Hook gets its sustainable lobsters from Maine and is a water kennel (or "pound") for lobsters. Many a roll misses the mark by skimping on the meat, but not at Red Hook Lobster Pound. No fillers—nothing but buttery, fresh-from-the sea lobster, with fully intact claws, served up with proper amounts of sauce, on the right kind of toasted bread. They have other lobster-infused (and fish-free) items on their menu, but you come here for the lobster roll, and maybe a side of the Cape Cod chips (salt and vinegar all the way).

THE GOOD FORK

#dinner #FusionDoneRight
#PorkDumplings
391 Van Brunt Street

A Red Hook institution, this restaurant serves American fare with a big Korean twist. This new-school mom-and-pop restaurant is run by husband-and-wife team Ben and Sohui. Ben is responsible for the rustic, wooden boat interior that he cobbled together himself, and Sohui cooks up a storm every day, using her Korean roots to flavor the comforting American menu. Fusion food is pretty easy to fuck up, but at Good Fork, they definitely know what they're doing. Their pork-and-chive dumplings alone have gotten enough press to set them apart. Their Korean steak and eggs come with savory kimchi rice that's rounded out with sweet apples and peppery arugula. They stick to local ingredients, and while the menu is short, each item strikes that perfect balance of flavors.

THE BALLFIELDS

#LatinStreetFoodParadise
#BirthAFoodBaby
155 Bay Street

What started as an operation to feed the people playing soccer on the field has become a food journey that many Brooklynites (and Anthony Bourdain) take every summer. Flanking one side of the baseball field in Red Hook is a mecca of Latin food stands. Not just Mexican taco stands (although those are there)—here you'll find Colombian (arepas and chiccarones!), Salvadoran (pupusas at El Olomega), and Guatemalan (Ochoa's ceviche) flavors (among others). You will need to fast the day prior to your pilgrimage.

◉ SEE AND DO

JALOPY THEATER AND SCHOOL OF MUSIC

#LiveMusic #free #fiddlers
315 Columbia Street

Where beards and suspenders come to learn the musical crafts of their times, the Jalopy is a music school during the day that'll teach you how to finger various strings and blow a bunch of reeds. At night, the theater holds shows. While most have a cover, "Roots and Rukus" is a free Wednesday-night show hosted by Feral Foster, a unique character who performs during the show. The well-curated show has different acts every time, but will always have some folky aspect to it. We once saw a sixty-five-year-old butch Venezuelan woman scream-sing (in sort of Spanish) about how vaginas screwed her over. You sit on church pews, a dollar per act is the expected donation, and you can get beer, wine, or tea up front. Everyone goes to the bar next door to keep the party going after the show.

WATERFRONT MUSEUM AND SHOWBOAT BARGE

#history #CoolDécor
290 Conover St., Pier 44

Inside an old, historic (but smelly) barge out on the Red Hook waterfront, this museum is all about transporting you to the world of the pre-technology shipping industry along the river. Back then, barges carried all kinds of great goods, like nuts and coffee, across long distances and waterfronts were thriving areas for the community. Now that things are airborne, the waterfront has lost its flare. The aim here is to restore that liveliness through preservation and education. Oh, and you get an awesome view of the Statue of Liberty.

🏪 SHOP

FREEBIRD BOOKS AND GOODS

#bookstore #NYCCulture
123 Columbia Street

A used bookstore on the Columbia waterfront, Freebird specializes in books about NYC culture and history. They carry a lot of lightly worn, used books (and accept donations), with a few new books in the mix. The kind of place where you'll come up on an obscure title from the '50s, Freebird is a cozy shop where you can roll up into a ball and lounge around with a glass of wine and a good book. Freebird likes to promote local writers to keep Brooklyn's creative lit scene alive, and they support Books Behind Bars, a program that provides reading material to prisoners. It's only open on weekends and is a bit of a trek from the train.

PARTYING

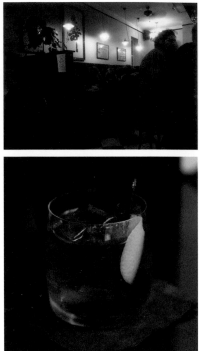

FORT DEFIANCE

#bar #coffee #brunch
365 Van Brunt Street

Since Hurricane Sandy hit, all of Red Hook bound together, and now everyone knows one another and shares everything. It may sound a little cultish, but after the ordeal that this waterfront hood went through, you can understand why. The local spot for everything from coffee to brunch to nice, strong cocktails is Fort Defiance. A really nice, homey, quirky place to grab an Irish coffee (often made by the owner/bartender) and some amazing deviled eggs. They throw a tiki party every Thursday night, and on Mondays there's a standing $12 beer-and-burger special. If you find yourself banging on their door the next morning, their brunch is killer and pairs well with a perfectly spicy Bloody Mary. Hit it from every angle to get a well-rounded idea of what Fort Defiance is all about.

RED HOOK BAIT & TACKLE
#bar #nautical #CheapBeer
320 Van Brunt Street

Although it might look like the Bait &
Tackle is owned by an eighty-year-old
hunting fisherman who's been hoarding his
knickknacks and taxidermied conquests
for years, the bar has only been open since
2004. Owned by two local dudes who met
drinking down the street, the bar maintains
a sense of humor about its ridiculous stuffed
bear, pillows on the ceiling, and plastic
duck décor. The beers here are cheap (as
low as $2!), you'll get to hang out with the
neighborhood dogs, and the couches in the
back are great for when your sea legs give
out. There's also an authentic "mustache
ride"; do with that knowledge what you will.

SUNNY'S BAR
#bar #OldSchool
253 Conover Street

When you're looking to step into a simpler
time of whiskey, bluegrass, and good
company, Sunny's is fiddlin' the night away
in Red Hook ready to entertain you and
your mustachioed friends. Their apple cider
is hard, the music live, and the décor old
and funky. Split up into different spaces to
accommodate chatty drinkers; and those
wishing to jam out to the music, this place
will rub your soul the right way. Sunny
and his bar have been around for years to
quench the locals' thirst for old-timey booze
and tunes, and even though its existence was
threatened by Sandy, the bar picked itself
up and got back to the business of creating
unforgettable experiences for all who dare
to trek out into no-subway territory.

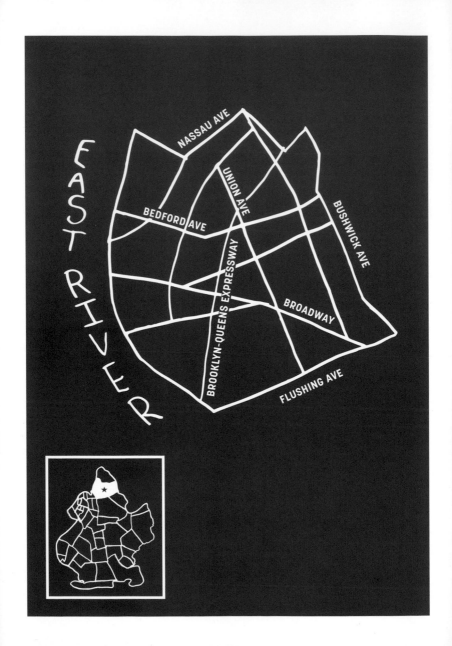

WILLIAMSBURG

No matter how much you like to hipster-hate, it's undeniable that Williamsburg is overflowing with little crafty shops, great restaurants, cafés, street art, and a young, sometimes obnoxious, local population. People here love bikes, brunches, and mustaches. The neighborhood lies on the East River waterfront, and every summer weekend the Brooklyn Flea rolls in with craft wares, antiques, and interesting vintage items. Smorgasburg, the food part of the Flea, keeps you full with a wide selection of vendors selling everything from lobster rolls to vegan sliders. At night, everyone gets shitty and goes wild at super dives and music venues. The streets often absorb house parties, and everything spills in a mass jumble of ironic T-shirts, glitter, and exposed side-boobs. Even though the ruckus reigns, Williamsburg has grown up some—with new, lofts and condos being built to draw an older, richer crowd—and while you'll still see sloppy Saturday-night drunks, suped-up baby strollers are trickling in.

NORTH SIDE

☕ COFFEE AND BAKERIES

BLUE BOTTLE COFFEE
#IcedCoffee #WestCoastImport #smores
160 Berry Street

When you come in here, you better not order a grande anything. At Blue Bottle, an Oakland, California import, coffee is dead serious. The proprietor made a still-standing promise to get your coffee from roasting to cup within no more than forty-eight hours. This spot answers the call of the hype by pumping out some refined coffee. If it's hot out, you must have a cup of their Kyoto cold brew, made by using some Japanese process that extracts like a milli drop per hour.

OTP Tip: Blue Bottle makes these Brooklyn bootleg s'mores, which sounds like you'll get a dime bag and a bullet on a graham cracker. In reality, it's a homemade graham cracker, layered with Mast Brothers chocolate, a puffy homemade marshmallow, and a splash of booze to bind it. You see it, you buy it, no questions.

EL BEIT
#coffee #backyard
158 Bedford Avenue

The standout beans here are from 49th Parallel, a fair trade company in Vancouver. Even though they're not locally sourced from some Brooklyn bearded man's backyard, they are indeed delicious. Get an espresso-based drink; they know what they're doing with these beans. El Beit also has a few crafty sandwiches and baked goods (try

any of the loaves) that get gobbled up by hungry, hungry hipsters by midday. Expect to hear some early '90s throwback jams, sometimes accompanied by impromptu singing. Their backyard is large and half covered, in case you need to escape sudden summer downpours.

MOMOFUKU
#dessert #CrackPie #FamousFood
253 Conover Street

We're gonna give it to you real straight and we're only gonna say it once, so listen carefully: There are few things in this entire universe that will make you feel as good as Crack Pie. Or Birthday Cake Truffles. Or Compost Cookies. Or, really, anything that the sweet tooth scientists at Momofuku Milk Bar make. There's so much we could say to convince you to go here, but we'll hold off. (More Crack Pie for us!)

ODDFELLOWS ICE CREAM CO.
#IceCream #CrazyFlavors
175 Kent Avenue

Most of Brooklyn's ice-cream makers seem to have moved toward isolating flavors and showcasing single ingredients. OddFellows took a left turn at the corner of weird and weirder and offers ice cream flavors like Manchego Pineapple and Thyme, Extra Virgin Olive Oil, and one infused with Guinness. Aside from being weirdos, OddFellows is great at nuancing bold flavors from their fresh, local ingredients and makes small batches of their interesting concoctions using Battenkill Valley Creamery milk. How did all this oddness come about? Well, the owners are a husband-and-wife team, and when the lady was pregnant, the dude told his cheffy friend about her crazy-ass cravings. These cravings were eventually captured in a pint of ice cream, and then expanded into a full-service ice-cream shop of oddities in June, 2013.

OSLO COFFEE ROASTERS
#espresso #ToGo
133-B Roebling Street

With locations all over NYC, Oslo has a cult following. Sure, their drip coffee is pretty good, but not foam-at-the-mouth spectacular. Perhaps the hype comes from the fact that the owner is from Seattle (aka the coffee capital of the United States). Regardless, if you're craving a well-pulled shot of espresso, stop in. Their iced drinks are also consistently strong. The shop itself, like other Oslo locations, is small and not very inviting.

THE BLUE STOVE
#bakery #pie #GreatGrandmasRecipes
415 Graham Avenue

Take a break from the Brooklyn grind and step into 1952. The Blue Stove is a coffee shop and bakery named after a blue wood stove on the back wall that once belonged to the owner's great-grandmother. That tribute to tradition is baked into her lovingly made pies that are served fresh every day. This place is overflowing with pie, and no matter what kooky flavors they concoct, the crust is always buttery and flakey, the way great-grandma used to make it. Their flavors change seasonally, but some knockouts are the Sour Cherry, the Burstin' with Blueberry Pie, and

the Black-Bottom Lemon Custard Pie. They also serve sweet and savory pastries, like the lunch-worthy Bacon Apple Cheddar Biscuit Sandwich and various pot pies.

TOBY'S ESTATE COFFEE
#coffee #FancyBeans #popular
126 N. 6th Street

Toby's is super strung-out on coffee and interior design. The window-walled shop is breathtaking and doubles as a roasting plant where all of their carefully sourced beans are taken to their full, crackity-brown brew potential. At Toby's, beans are treated like fine wine, and you can have your coffee made using several extraction methods. Each coffee bears a "notes" description, and while our palates aren't all that refined, each variety of bean does have a distinct flavor. They have a few choice breakfast items made in-house and pastries made by local bakers. The design matches the craftiness of their coffee, with low-hanging lamps, huge decorative shelves, and clean wood and metal furniture. This place is super popular on weekends, and seating is hard to find (even during off times).

 # EAT

CARACAS AREPAS BAR

#Venezuelan #arepas #LunchSpecial
#rum

291 Grand Street

No one can love the arepa quite like Caracas Arepa Bar. Their arepas are tenderly filled with combos of meat, cheese, and veggies, all bursting with slow-cooked flavor. Experience the excellent variety by ordering a few arepas, like the De Pabellón (shredded beef, sweet plantains, white salty cheese, and black beans) and the La De Pernil (roasted pork shoulder, tomato, and spicy mango sauce). The lunch special ($8.50) is fantastic; you get a soup or salad with whatever arepa you'd like. While most places give you some throwaway salad, Caracas uses a high-quality balsamic dressing on theirs and breaks up the texture with the best hearts of palm you've ever had. One arepa might sound like a snack, but somehow these are so filling (with a slight crunch) that one will keep you full for hours. The whole place is colorful and made warm by the chunks of wood used to decorate the walls. Make sure to visit Roneria Caracas, the rum bar up front, and hit them up for bottomless mimosa brunch ($15) on the weekends.

CHAMPS

#diner #vegan #brunch

174 Ainslie Street

Craving a milk shake without the milk? How 'bout an egg scramble, hold the eggs? This 100 percent vegan diner and bakery is as cute as it is free of animal products. It's one of those places you can bring omnivores and shock them by the awesome vegan food.

There are pancakes and benedicts, French toast and rancheros, basically everything you know and love, with more love and less meat.

OTP Tip: Meatless lovers from far and wide come out to feast for brunch, so if you like getting a table in a timely manner, get here early on the weekends or swing by Champs Junior, a counter in Greenpoint serving up the same guilt-free eats in a smaller setting.

EL ALMACEN

#dinner #brunch #Argentine #steak

557 Driggs Avenue

Great for both dinner and brunch, El Almacen serves the kind of food you wish you could make at home. With a mostly Argentine menu, come to this place for meat (pour on the chimichurri by the bottle) or give into the goodness of the dulce de leche French toast. All of their products are mindfully and locally sourced, and meticulously prepared. Obviously, you need to order from the parilla (the grill), and while all the options are phenomenal (skirt steak served in interesting vessels), they do get pricey. If you're looking to get mind-blown for cheaper, get the against-the-rules avocado fries ($6) and sit around in their romantic interior, thinking about why you've never had the balls to deep-fry battered avocado slices.

ENDLESS SUMMER TRUCK

#StreetFood #GringoTacos #burritos #HotDudes

(usually around) 152 Metropolitan Avenue

This taco isn't your answer to authentic Mexican street food, but it is something special in its own right. Sitting outside of Skinny Dennis on Metropolitan Avenue, their prime parking spot is perfect for when you're craving something spicy after a night of partying. While we've definitely indulged during the day, Endless Summer is what drunk food dreams are made of. Their tacos are $2.50-$3.00, full of flavor, wrapped in locally made tortillas, perfectly garnished, and the chorizo in that bad boy ain't fucking around. The burritos are stuffed with rice, beans, meat, onion, and cilantro. This truck isn't run by Mexicans but by young, good-looking dudes cooking up the stuff they want to eat when they're a little booze-happy. The menu includes a good deal of vegetarian options (with seitan) to satisfy the late-night cravings of all who frolic around these parts.

FETTE SAU

#BBQ #FamousFood

354 Metropolitan Avenue

Fette Sau (or "fat pig") is the mother lode when it comes to Brooklyn BBQ. Seriously, no trip to Brooklyn is complete without dining at this a la carte, oh-so-perfectly smoked meat and whiskey joint. Housed in a converted auto repair garage, this place retains some of the repurposed grit that put Williamsburg on the map. Snag a seat at the bar or one of the communal tables for the full experience. Zagat named Fette Sau the best BBQ in New York City for three years in a row, which means you need to get there early to get in. They don't take reservations, but we forgive 'em because their meat is so good you can smell the smoke a block away.

FORNINO

#pizza #OldSchool
187 Bedford Avenue

Gourmet pizza places are a dime a dozen in New York, but Fornino may be the oldest old-school one that still makes the grade. The crust is perfectly crispy, ingredients are perfectly proportioned, and though its main location is literally on the hippest corner of the hippest neighborhood in the hippest city in the country, its laid-back vibe is more reminiscent of Papa John's than Papa Bloomberg. The Tartufo, made with ricotta and black winter truffle, is totally worth the extra cash.

GRAHAM AVENUE MEATS AND DELI

#MonsterItalianSandwiches #cheap
445 Graham Avenue

You like ridiculously huge sandwiches? Well, we've got just the place to serve all your gluttonous needs. Downing a full sandwich at Graham Avenue will put you out of commission for a few hours. Get the Godfather and get it spicy. This sandwich contains an entire Italian pantry and fridge worth of ingredients (notably, mortadella, sopressata, peppers, Parmesan, provolone, and the right amounts of vinegar, oil, and spicy condiments) lovingly crammed onto a semolina roll. Somehow, all of this Italian stuff never fails to strike the right balance of sour and spicy, meaty and cheesy, and once you unhinge your jaw to get that sucker closer to your throat, you'll understand why people travel for miles to this small, out of the way deli.

MABLE'S SMOKEHOUSE AND BANQUET HALL

#BBQ #Oklahoma #FritoPie
44 Berry Street

Meghan and Jeff, a husband-and-wife team, built this place with their bare hands and named it after Jeff's grandmother. The space is huge and open, with BBQ-appropriate wooden communal tables. They've really got the Southern hospitality thing down, and their food is the epitome of comfort. Their DeLuxe Platter ($32.95), with your choice of three succulent meats and sides, will feed a family of four. The brisket is luscious, the ribs will get all over your face, and the Bet's Best Potato Salad really lives up to its name. Mable's is Oklahoma-style BBQ served at an affordable price (when you take portions into account), and they have Frito pie . . . as in they put chili and cheese inside a bag of Fritos.

THE MEATBALL SHOP

#meatballs #customizable
#IceCreamSandwiches
170 Bedford Avenue

According to the proprietors of this joint (a Brooklyn outpost of popular Manhattan locations), balls are much better when they're slathered in Parmesan cream or tomato sauce and served on a toasted brioche bun. Eating here is like a choose-your-eating adventure—the interactive menu requires you to put a check next to the kind of balls you want, the sauce, and the delivery method into your mouth (sliders, heroes, etc.). With ball jokes running throughout, they've got spicy pork, beef, chicken, veggie, and special balls (which can be anything from lamb to jambalaya balls). The sauces (mushroom gravy!) are what make these balls really shine. The available sides are great, and if you're getting an "everything but the kitchen sink" salad, you can transform your balls into "family jewels" by throwing an egg on top for an extra buck. You know what goes great with balls? Ice-cream sandwiches. Especially when you get to pick the cookie and the ice cream.

OASIS
#falafel #cheap #DrunkFood
161 N. 7th Street

When you find yourself drunk and hungry in Williamsburg late at night, Oasis will be your shining beacon of hope. It may not be the fanciest falafel around, but it hits that drunk spot for super cheap. Don't get us wrong, the food here is fresh and delicious, but then again we've never had it sober. Their shawarma is juicy and flavorful, but the falafel platter is where it's at. For under $10, you get several crispy large falafel, mounds of freshly made salads from the counter, tangy tahini sauce, pitas, a dolma, and creamy homemade hummus. Usually stuffed to the brim with packs of party people, Oasis is known to cure even the worst case of the hangry drunks.

PATES & TRADITIONS
#French #crêpes #CountryDécor
52 Havemeyer Street

Get all French fancy on yourself and come

here to practice your phlegmy pronunciation of "croissant." Featuring classic French cooking, Pates & Traditions is best known for their crêpes. Decked out in little French details, like mini-curtains on the walls and pictures of potted plants (and actual potted plants), this place will put you in a carefree mood. As far as the crêpes are concerned, these aren't just dainty little sweet things. A hearty combo of sweet and savory, La Berger is a square crêpe filled with goat cheese, caramelized onions, and figs. For more bite, you can get La Normande, a meaty crêpe with chicken, mushrooms braised in white wine, and Swiss with herbs. And because we can all stuff another crêpe down the gullet, finish off with something sweet perhaps with Nutella all over it. The weekends get pretty packed and the place isn't very big.

ST. ANSELM
#dinner #TreatYourself #WildMeats #bacon
355 Metropolitan Avenue

Like dining inside a fancy old gin bottle covered in saws, the restaurant is dark but fresh-feeling, and if you're in the mood to eat big, St. Anselm will hook you up. They know how to traditionally prepare your meats but revel in their ability to shock you with a little twist. Its open kitchen creates things like gigantic (42-ounce) axe-handle rib eyes, whole roasted trout, head-on tea-brined whole chicken, and bacon cut so thick it looks like a severed finger. They don't hold back on the butter, and the creamed spinach is something special. Come here for meat, well-treated veggies (pan-fried mashed potatoes!), interesting specials (keep an ear out for kangaroo meat), great wine, and bacon-sprinkled ice cream.

WILD GINGER
#vegan #AsianFusion #LunchSpecial
212 Bedford Avenue

Most Asian-fusion places are confused, and everything ends up tasting like brown sauce from a can. Wild Ginger not only nails fusion but also ups the ante by making everything vegan. Taking the meat and dairy out of Asian isn't too hard, and Wild Ginger proves that there are a lot of flavorful things you can do with veggies and alternative proteins. Their lunch specials are a really good deal. For around $8, you get miso soup, a crispy fried spring roll, perfectly cooked brown rice speckled with al dente soybeans, and an entrée chosen from the fifteen or so options. There's a good mix of "fake" meat options, like mango soy protein and black pepper seitan, but also full-on veggie options like yam and pumpkin tempura. Outside of the lunch menu, there are a ton of interesting appetizers, salads, and noodle dishes. Although it may sound like the grossest thing on the menu, the boiled spinach with ponzu appetizer is really something unique.

OTP Tip: When ordering, stick with the fake land creatures, as Wild Ginger hasn't quite perfected veggie "seafood."

SEE AND DO

BROOKLYN ART LIBRARY (SKETCHBOOK LIBRARY)

#art #stories #interactive
#WeirdWaytoSpendAnHour

103A N. 3rd Street

An interesting concept that's part museum, part art project, with a hint of voyeuristic charm. The idea is that you sign up for a "library card" at the computer in the back. Once you get your card, you can check out two sketchbooks. The sketchbooks are randomly selected for you from the jam-packed shelves based on your responses to a couple computer-prompted questions. Once your order is placed, you take a seat and the clerk will bring you two sketchbooks from the library's collection (displayed all along every wall in the place). Sometimes you'll get a cool illustrated story, other times a depressing cancer tale. It's kind of a hit or miss, but you can go back and get as many books as you want once you're done with the initial two. The cool thing is that anyone in the world can participate. For $25, you get a basic notebook, and it's up to you to decorate, write in, and mess with it in any way you please. You then send it back to the library and it becomes part of the collection.

BUNNYCUTLET GALLERY

#ArtGallery #cartoons #superheros

158 Roebling Street

An open white space that fills up with colorful cartoons and gets jammed with people every opening day, Bunnycutlet is all about pop art with a nerdy comic book flair. The front is wrapped in a cartoony octopus, the back room houses all kinds of dorky dorkdom, and their exhibited artists always bring some Yoda, superhero, cat portraiture, and carney exuberance to the art party. Their group shows are really fun and a mash-up of all kinds of weirdo art. Owned and operated by a former animator, Bunnycutlet is the kind of gallery you wish existed in high school.

EIGHT OF SWORDS TATTOO

#ArtGallery #custom

115 Grand Street

Both a tattoo shop and an art gallery, Eight of Swords is where you go to get wildly inspired. They hold receptions for frequently rotating art shows, and if the art doesn't get your thoughts bubbling, the free wine should do the trick. This place is all about working with you to create custom pieces, and the artists here have impressive portfolios. (Seriously, check out Betty Rose!) They also have a pretty incredible selection of locally designed jewelry, should you be more into punching holes than getting ink. Overall, a superclean and art-centric shop.

FLYRITE TATTOO

#SailorJerry #HighlyExperienced

429 Metropolitan Avenue

Probably the most popular tattoo shop in Brooklyn, Flyrite is in the heart of Williamsburg right next to the BQE, and the place has poked its fair share of skin in the last fifteen years. Owned by a famed tattoo super star from NYC's tattoo underground, Elio Espana. Flyrite is home to some of the most professional and extensively trained tattoo artists out there. The shop is all about the art and tattoo culture. Run by Steven Huie, who's great at large-scale, colorful tats, Flyrite employs artists who will help you create (or come up with) whatever you want to stick onto your body. While Flyrite does accommodate spur-of-the-moment walk-ins, the place is really busy, so it's best to make a reservation (with a $100 deposit that goes toward the final cost of your tattoo).

NITEHAWK CINEMA

#MovieTheater #FancyFood #booze

136 Metropolitan Street

Let's face it, going out to a movie lost its charm the minute Netflix made its way into our lives. But Nitehawk has survived because it's more than just a movie theater. Here you will find gastrofare tailored to the movie on-screen, craft beers, and themed cocktails, all served while you watch. Their preshows aren't used as an opportunity for Coca-Cola to get you to the concession stand; instead, they screen relevant short films and clips to round out your moviegoing experience. Movie tickets are $11, there's a table and menu at every seat, and you can order reasonably priced, delicious food and drinks before or during the movie. Nitehawk fought hard to overturn the archaic laws that prohibited booze in theaters and is doing

their best to turn the obsolete activity into something a lot more fun.

PIEROGI 2000

#ArtGallery #BoilerRoom

177 N. 9th Street

Any place that names their establishment after a delicious European dumpling has to be good. Pierogi is the kind of gallery you visit with zero worry that you'll be stuck looking at someone's broad interpretation of abstract art. Here, they bring in the thought-provoking stuff that's worth your visit. In addition to a proper gallery space, they've got a huge boiler room (which used to be an actual boiler room) where they set up large installations and hold screenings. Also, they're a short walk away from super-Polski Greenpoint, should you want to move the experience of pierogi from your eyes to your mouth.

SAVED TATTOO

#GoodLocation #ScottCampbell

426 Union Avenue

Scott Campbell is the famous guy at this place, so if you want something done by him, you will have to wait in line with the others. In our opinion, everyone at Saved is extremely talented, and if you get too itchy for a tat to wait, talk to Michelle Tarantelli. Girl's got some skill. Her tats are very detailed, colorful, and full of character. Saved is in the middle of Williamsburg, so if you can't get inspiration inside the studio, take a peek around the block; chances are the covered passersby will get your tattoo thought bubbles a-poppin'.

TATTOO CULTURE

#creative #InternationalGuestArtists
129 Roebling Street

You come to this shop because you want a certain artist to draw whatever they want (or stylize your idea) onto your skin. Tattoo Culture is comprised of two resident artists, Gene and Brian, whose styles are completely different. Brian's art is a lot more traditional, and Gene does crazy paint splatters, super precise thin-line designs, and trippy, dripping animals, landscapes, and surrealist pieces. Noon (a guest artist) is a French guy with a very distinct boxy, geometric, cartoonish style that we get all worked up about. If you think tattoos are more about getting cool art, then Tattoo Culture is absolutely up your alley.

THE CITY RELIQUARY

#museum #oddities #NYCulture
370 Metropolitan Avenue

Dedicated to collecting and displaying the little pieces that make this borough special, the museum is a great way to get a glimpse into NYC's recent past. When you walk through the shanty doors, you'll notice knickknacks like pre-MetroCard subway tokens, building fragments, and other obscure items. The museum's mission is to inspire the community to document the world around them through found artifacts and other objects of meaning. As such, they hold community events like "Show and Tell" and throw parties in the yard to support local businesses (like ice-cream and doughnut shops). The place smells a little weird, but adds a new dimension to your understanding of this interesting borough.

THE FRONT ROOM GALLERY

#ArtGallery #MultiMedia #merch
147 Roebling Street

The Front Room exhibits clever, witty art of all types, with a focus on video, audio, and digital art. Some of what they put on display is conceptual, some straightforward, and some will make you go, "Oh shit, is that an arty Porta-Potty?" The gallery also supports "multiples and editions," a project that explores art's connection to money through the reproduction of artistic items, some that have functions beyond art (like an herb garden), others that are purely reproductions of original works with no non-art functions. This basically means they've got a gift shop with things that say, "Fuck you for buying anything."

YOGA TO THE PEOPLE

#yoga #sweat #cheap
211 N. 11th Street

Yoga to the People is a cheap way to get bendy. Classes are held at all times of the day and the Williamsburg studio is airy and comfortable. While Power Vinyasa Flow is a good class to take for a sweat, the ultimate workout is the hot-yoga class. Comparable to Bikram yoga, this class will make you sweat like a llama wearing a sweater in the Sahara. What you'll need: $10, a towel, a bottle of water, a yoga mat (which can be rented at $2 apiece), and a willingness to hurt and like it.

SHOP

ARTISTS AND FLEAS MARKET

#ArtisanShowcase #LocalDesigners
70 N. 7th Street

Less of a flea market, more of a showcase of artisan wares, Artists and Fleas is full of really cool, trendsetting finds. It's much pricier than anything you'll find at your typical yard sale, but every item is unique and made with artistic flare. You'll find a lot of repurposed metal and wood, cool prints on shirts and other goods, unisex jewelry, journals, bike accessories, eco-bags, and wearable vintage. It's the kind of place you go to buy that one special person (maybe yourself) a unique piece that'll woo them with your good taste.

BROOKLYN CHARM

#JewelryStore #indie #customizable
145 Bedford Avenue

Instead of buying something "special" at the airport to commemorate your trip, head to Brooklyn Charm for a piece of unique jewelry that you can continue to build every time you come back. As the name hints, this shop sells charms and the necklaces, bracelets, or other adornments on which those charms are mounted. An interactive jewelry experience, the store urges you to be the designer. They have a large menu of items and services, and you get to choose the metals, chains, charms, and rings. They carry cool things like the fifty states charms, little coins that say ridiculous things, and all kinds of animal shapes. The store will also engrave anything for you, and if you're a crafty SOB, you can just buy the materials and put the jewelry together yourself to avoid the service fees. It's not cheap, but it's fun and unique.

BROOKLYN FLEA

#FleaMarket #LocalDesigners
#tchotchkes #furniture #food
Summer: 50 Kent Ave (between N. 11th and 12th Streets)
Winter: 80 N. 5th Street

A huge operation with a few locations around Brooklyn, we think this market has the perfect amount of fleas. The Williamsburg version of the Flea is the largest and busiest. While the vendors are similar between locations, this Flea comes with a waterfront view in the summer. The goods offered are on a broad spectrum of spanking new (featuring local designers) to filthy old (we saw WWII long johns once). Many things (like jewelry, new fashions, vintage eyewear, and furniture) are priced pretty high, but there's room to dig for deals. If you get hungry picking through the pieces, there are a heaping handful of food vendors to revive your thrifting spirits. Grab a fresh crispy dosa from Dosa Royal and continue picking through people's stuff like you mean business.

Smorgasburg

From small snacks to full-on meals served fresh from their respective stands, Smorgasburg (winter: 80 N. 5th Street; summer: East River Park) is where you go to try a little of everything from some of the most innovative food hawkers in Brooklyn. During the summer, Smorgasburg cozies up to the Williamsburg waterfront (11:00 a.m. to 6:00 p.m.) and you can enjoy a food-stall-gathered lunch on the picnic tables outside. The vendor list is always changing to showcase the best bites around. You can get a snappy dog from Brooklyn Bangers, amazing (vegan) Ethiopian from Bunna, slow-roasted porchetta, an all-fruit People's Pop Popsicle, and a strong brew from Brooklyn Roasting Company. If you see Outer Borough here, you must get their beef rolled up in a scallion pancake. From cured meats to lobster rolls to pupusas, the selection will make you feel like you've won the food lottery.

5 FREE THINGS TO DO IN WILLIAMSBURG

In Williamsburg, free doesn't mean boring. Release your wallet from the suffocating grip of pay-to-play and enjoy the freedom of free.

FREE TO BROWSE

BROOKLYN NIGHT BAZAAR

A giant night market, the Brooklyn Night Bazaar (165 Banker Street) goes off every Friday and Saturday night in a warehouse between Williamsburg and Greenpoint, with unique vendors like well-curated, repurposed vintage clothing, to funky locally designed jewelry and gift items like tiny dioramas and all kinds of finds.

FREE WORKOUT

MCCARREN PARK POOL

Every summer, the heat and muck push everyone in the direction of McCarren Pool. While it's known for midday lounging, the pool is huge, and getting a few laps in when the crowd is thinner will be a nice workout. Entry is free, but you must bring a padlock (or you can't get in), towel, and legit swimsuit (and not much more).

Bonus: McCarren Park hosts Sunscreen every summer, where free movies like *Back to the Future* and *The Big Lebowski* are thrown up on a screen in the park to be enjoyed with a Solo Cup and a roll in the grass.

FREE BEER TOUR

BROOKLYN BREWERY

A well-known local brewery, Brooklyn Brewery's actual headquarters is right in the middle of Williamsburg (79 N. 11th Street), and they happily give tours of the facilities (every half hour from 1:00 to 5:00 p.m. on weekends or by appointment on weekdays).

FREE MUSIC

PETE'S CANDY STORE

The only candy served here is booze. The large drinking room in the front funnels into a narrow old street car with a backlit performance stage in the back. This setup makes Pete's Candy Store (79 Lorimer Street) a great (free) music venue with live music every night. As if putting on a show every night isn't enough, the first Monday of every month, Pete's holds the Williamsburg Spelling Bee. If you get out-worded in the first round, the backyard is a nice, quiet, colorful place to figure out how to spell d-e-f-e-a-t.

FREE CHOCOLATE

MAST BROTHERS CHOCOLATE

You've never seen two people take chocolate as seriously as the bearded Mast Brothers (111 N. 3rd Street). They source their cocoa beans so lovingly that they practically cuddle with them to extract the chocolaty goodness, then wrap them in heavyweight paper with prints designed uniquely for each flavor. This isn't that Hershey's bullshit; the chocolate flavors here are dark and bitter, with that perfect snap. They lay out free samples of each bar, so if you need just a little fix, have a bite (although it's impossible not to get reeled into paying for a pricey bar).

BUFFALO EXCHANGE
#ThriftShop #NewStyles #vintage
504 Driggs Avenue

Unlike typical thrift shops that smell like the mothiest of your grandma's old tweed coats, this shop buys mostly new styles that are in great shape and ready for you to rock. Buffalo is a countrywide chain that has two locations in Brooklyn. Since the stores buy from mostly locals (and they keep local shoppers in mind when creating the inventory), each shop location uniquely reflects the style of the surrounding neighborhood. The Williamsburg store has a lot of indie designer brands, weird DIY shirts, and quirky footwear. A unisex shopping experience, go to Buffalo when you have a little time to dig around for goods. They keep the pricier stuff behind the counter, and there's always a kick-ass 50 percent off rack.

CROSSROADS
#ThriftShop #NewStyles
135 N. 7th Street

The BK outpost of a countrywide chain, Crossroads started recycling fashions back in '91 in San Francisco. At any given time, you'll see people with huge bags of cool-looking things at the buying counter. The layout is such that the new items are displayed up front and the secondhand stuff is hung on long racks that funnel into the fitting rooms in the back. This setup makes it so you get sucked in right from the get-go. You'll touch a few shirts and then before you know it, you've got fifteen things on your arm that total no more than fifty bucks.

ROUGH TRADE NYC
#RecordStore #vinyls #turntables #lounge
64 N. 9th Street

An updated record store, this UK Import specializes in vinyl and CDs, but it also carries all kinds of music equipment and accessories and has listening stations, a turntable, and a chilling lounge that overlooks the entire, massive space. While some of their items are kind of on the expensive side and you won't find that weird shit that only five people consider actual music, it is an interesting shop to browse, listen to music, or read some music mags and books. Rough Trade also hosts in-store concerts showcasing local artists, and if all this isn't enough, there's a couple Ping-Pong tables to get you pumped.

MONK
#ThriftShop #Vintage #digging
496 Driggs Avenue

This place is crotchety and will put your digging skills to the test. Not the sort of place where you go to find a nice pair of Levi's, but it's not totally unlikely that you'll stumble onto a pair during your search. Good for those with an open mind when it comes to fashion, this place has a bunch of unique pieces scattered about. There are bins and boxes with scarves, gloves, tights, and other interesting accessories. The circular racks hold the kinds of things that fit into the "one man's trash is another man's treasure" cliché. All the digging will always pay off as their prices are super low. They have a dollar rack outside but it's usually treasure-free garbage.

THE MEAT HOOK

#SpecialtyFood #butcher #OliveOil #sausages #workshops

100 Frost Street

The Meat Hook is a new-age butcher, and walking into the shop you'll be surrounded by all kinds of products, kitchen tools, condiments, produce, jars, and other goods meant to turn you into a kitchen genius. A whole (grass-fed) animal butcher shop, the meat department is stocked to the teeth with every cut of beef, chicken, pork, and game. They make classy sausages (like bratwurst, spicy Italian, and several types of chorizo) and trashy sausages (like the Bacon Cheeseburger and French Onion—their take on French onion soup in sausage form). Their imported balsamic vinegar and olive oils, available on tap, are absolutely incredible. They carry all kinds of rare spices, and if you've got a food-obsessed friend, the Meat Hook is great for unique edible gifts. They hold classes and workshops next door at the Brooklyn Kitchen to help you become a better meat eater and food maker. It's expensive, but the staff is super knowledgeable, the goods are impeccable, and you can always just lurk around for a few hours to get inspired without spending much.

WILLIAMSBURG MINI-MALL

#SmallBusinessCollabo #gadgets #books #clothes #UniqueGifts

218 Bedford Avenue

You won't find an H&M or Victoria's Secret in this mall. Rather, this mini-mall houses quirky indie shops that include MeMe Antenna (a gift shop with NYC stuff like postcards and totes but also weird tchotchkes), Dijital Fix (a store with electronic gadgets, cool headphones, and speakers), Spoonbill & Sugartown Booksellers (a grungy bookshop), and others. It's fun to just walk around inside to get away from Bedford Avenue for a minute and browse the oddities that find their way into the short hallway separating the stores.

FUN FACT

The first air conditioner was installed in Williamsburg. If you go there in August, you'll know why.

PARTYING

ALLIGATOR LOUNGE
#bar #dive #FreePizza
600 Metropolitan Avenue

Let's say, theoretically, you're down to your last $5—you can A) cry, or B) grab a beer and a personal brick-oven pizza with $1 left to tip your bartender. With the purchase of a drink, you get a ticket for your own personal pizza pie—it's not the best pizza in the world, but it's not terrible (and it's fucking free, so quit complaining). Ladies, your lucky night is Thursday, when well drinks are $4—and, dudes, this is the perfect opportunity to "splurge" on your main squeeze, with money to spare for a game of Skee-Ball in the back.

BARCADE
#bar #arcade
388 Union Avenue

If you teleported to a rich, cool dude's garage in the late '70s/early '80s, it may look something like Barcade (minus the polyester). The only thing better than the forty-three old-school video games lining Barcade's walls are the twenty-seven taps of craft beer behind the bar. Think you can beat the reigning Frogger or Donkey Kong high scorers? Throw back an IPA and a shot of whiskey and give that joystick a tug.

BA'SIK
#bar #cheap #cocktails
323 Graham Avenue

Sometimes you get the urge to splurge; and then you open your wallet and realize it's nearly empty. Don't fret—put on your fancy-pants and get your ass to Ba'sik. The vibe is as chilled as the tasty, custom cocktails and the vintage/modern/industrial décor is sophisticated without being douchey. Stop by on Sunday night for a Poppa's Pride (yummy bourbon drink) and take in a little Gypsy Jazz.

BROOKLYN BOWL
#LiveMusic #bowling #FriedChicken
61 Wythe Avenue

Wouldn't it be cool if there was a kick-ass music venue where you could also bowl? A place that had an amazing bar and food from power purveyor Blue Ribbon inside? Brooklyn Bowl's on it! Okay, so truth is: It's kinda pricey to bowl here. But, time it right and you get to see a show while hitting mad strikes! Knock down some pins while knocking back a few fresh-from-the-source Brooklyn Brewery beers. And, the fried chicken is so good it's famous—not just famous by our standards, but these wings have been on TV 'n' shit; they're so good. You don't have to bowl to eat or drink here, so if you don't feel like throwing balls in the gutter, just stop by for a drink and a dance party.

CAMEO
#bar #cafe #MusicVenue #DJSets
93 N. 6th Street

Cameo's alter ego is "Loving Cup," and during the day it's a decent café with food. As the day fades into night, the cup gets filled with the kind of love that gets you drunk and urges you to stumble into the back room, where you'll find a really trippy white paper art/light installation on the ceiling that'll give you vertigo. Sometimes a mediocre DJ will be trying out a new set, other times you'll find Sharon Van Etten hanging out playing guitar. There's a little lean-to bar back there and the cover depends on the act. If you hate music but love laughing, *The Big Terrific*, a free comedy show that goes down every Wednesday, will win you over with its fart jokes.

CHARLESTON
#bar #dive #FreePizza
174 Bedford Avenue

It's easy to forget that you might contract airborne hepatitis when you're drinking cheap-as-fuck drinks and free personal pizzas. If you're trying to impress a date, do not bring them here. If you're trying to impress your homeless friend, or if you only have $5 to your name, we found you a new local spot. It's dingy, grimy, and perfect for when showering seems like an impossible feat.

CUBANA SOCIAL
#bar #brunch #mojitos #empanadas #rum
70 N. 6th Street

Right next to the Music Hall of Williamsburg, this place will draw you in with its open industrial interior and sexy Cuban vibe. The aim here is to bring back the feel of old Havana and remix it in a Brooklyn setting. They've got great mojitos ($10), their Cubano is stuffed with eight-hour-roasted pork, ham, Swiss, and perfect pickles, and you can get three empanadas for ten bucks. They do live Cuban jazz on Saturdays, offer a great weekend brunch when you're sick of the regular benedicts and pancakes, and are a good preshow rum flight ($15-$18) stop.

GLASSLANDS GALLERY
#venue #shows #DanceParties
289 Kent Avenue

While Glasslands is a smallish venue, they've gotten very popular on the "it" list of places cool bands want to play. As such, Glasslands gets to pick the best and grungiest bands around and bring them out from the Brooklyn shadows. This won't be like a Beyoncé concert; the cave-like space is set up for indie shows and the sound is gritty but good. The cover varies depending on the act (about $10 unless it's a big name), the three unisex bathrooms are a popular waiting-in-line/puking spot, and the bar is cash only. The kind of intimate place where you can smell whatever the stage is cooking, Glasslands is a good, sweaty party time.

KNITTING FACTORY BROOKLYN
#LiveMusic #ComedyShows #CheapBeers
361 Metropolitan Avenue

Although a fairly new kid on the Brooklyn block (it moved from its Manhattan location in 2009), the Knitting Factory has been a fixture music venue in NYC since 1987. There are two very different experiences to be had here. The first begins in the front room, a regular ol' bar filled with peeps suckin' down PBRs at picnic tables, trying to talk over loud music. The second experience happens in the back room, where bands and comedians you've actually heard of play for pretty dirt cheap. The venue only holds three hundred people, so there's not a bad seat (or place to stand) in the house. And, aside from the fact that you have to drink them out of plastic cups, drinks ($4-$6 beers) are fairly cheap considering it's a music venue.

MACRI PARK

#bar #backyard #dancing
462 Union Avenue

Right across the street from the Lorimer Street L/Metropolitan Avenue G interchange, this spot funnels in crowds looking to drink the minute they get off the train. While the indoor area is big enough and decorated with chili pepper Christmas lights, the big draw is the backyard, where communal tables help you get friendly with other pregamers and make plans for the night to come. Sometimes they'll bust out the old-school jams to incite impromptu dance parties and throw some silent Bruce Lee on the tele.

MAISON PREMIERE

#bar #absinthe
298 Bedford Avenue

With one of the largest selections of absinthe in New York, Maison Premiere is a great place to escape reality for a bit. OK kids, this place is very expensive if you don't do it right. Don't come here starving or if you're a raging alcoholic. Do come here to sample the unique hallucinogenic drink ($10-$17 each), served up proper with a sugar cube and chilled water. To complement your mind trip, get a few chilled (East or West Coast) oysters. While each little sea sucker will cost you close to $3 during peak hours, if you pop in Monday through Friday from four

to seven, you can get them for $1-1.25 each. This place draws huge happy-hour crowds (why aren't these people working?!). They'll *sometimes* honor reservations for happy hour, or just get there before 5:00 p.m.

MUSIC HALL OF WILLIAMSBURG

#LiveMusic #BigShows
66 N. 6th Street

Music Hall of Williamsburg is owned by Bowery Presents and is the first cousin to Bowery Ballroom in Manhattan. If you've never been to Bowery Ballroom and this name-dropping means nothing to you, just know that MHOW is one of the best places in NYC to see a show. For starters, it's small. Which means you can stand anywhere, including the balcony, and feel like you're onstage. There are two bars: one when you walk in, and one upstairs in the back (check out the Shepard Fairey mural while you're up there). The sound is amazing, which is why every indie band you could possibly name has played here. Old New Yorkers love to reminisce about CBGB's and Max's Kansas City—one day we'll be reminiscing about how many insane shows we saw at MHOW.

OUTPUT

#club #NoPhotos #dancing
74 Wythe Avenue

If all you want to do is dance, Output is a legit club that's all about the music. There is no bottle service and nobody takes pictures every thirty seconds (Output doesn't allow photos). You come here to dance hard to bigger-name house/electronica shows, and Output's sound system makes it an incredible experience. That said, it's pricey to party. The cover, depending on the night, averages $20-$25, the drinks are $10-$12, and if you're here in the winter, there is a mandatory $3 coat check. The right way to do Output is to go in the summer, pregame like a pro, hit the club lines outside around 10:00 p.m., take a big breath on the rooftop terrace once you're in, and then dance until you fracture a few toes.

RADEGAST HALL & BIERGARTEN

#bar #BeerHall #LiveMusic #sausages
113 N. 3rd Street

Stein for stein, this beer garden is quite impressive. A large, brick-walled indoor space with requisite beer hall communal tables, Radegast feels like it could be outdoors in some German festival but happens to be in the heart of Williamsburg. Don't skimp on the essentials. Come here with a group on a Thursday for their $5 half-liter special, with which you get a free brat. Don't stop at the sausage; get a couple of big, satisfying pretzels with spicy mustard as well. When you smell the grill, tack on more snappy-skinned sausages, a couple more pitchers, and listen to the sweet jams of live jazz strumming every day. A place you commit to for at least a few hours, Radegast has everything you need for a German good time.

ROSEMARY'S (GREENPOINT TAVERN)

#bar #GrandmaRun
#StyrofoamCupBeers
188 Bedford Avenue

We love bars run by old people. At Rosemary's, Grandma shoves thirty-two ounces of Styrofoam-outfitted beer down your throat for about $4 a pop. The deep end of a dive bar, Rosemary's is decorated with items you may find in your parents' basement. We're talking Christmas lights, art project leftovers from third grade, and dingy fake flowers your mom "planted" to spruce up the

yard. If you're lucky enough to catch Rosemary behind the bar, you're in for a good laugh. While getting her attention is difficult (possibly because she's somewhere in her seventies) and her mood fluctuates between pissed-off and annoyed, Rosemary has been doing this for more than fifty-five long years, and the woman doesn't fuck around. As for the patrons of this fine establishment, they range from drunken ex-convicts to hipsters pretending their trust funds have run out.

SKINNY DENNIS

#bar #Southern #AdultFrozenCoffee
152 Metropolitan Avenue

Set up to either make fun of the Southern transplants in the area or to genuinely give them something to cling to, Skinny Dennis is a loud, hillbilly-esque type bar that plays country, bluegrass, and other tunes that frequently include the fiddle. It's a dive of the kindest kind. They have a picture of Willie Nelson behind the bar, the drinks are not only extra large but super cheap (and sometimes strong), and they hook you up with warm peanuts in appreciation of your patronage. If you want to get real sloppy with it, get a "Willie's Frozen Coffee," a blend of ice cream, bourbon, and coffee grounds squeezed out of a churning soft-serve machine.

SPIKE HILL
#bar #DarkBooths #LiveMusic
184–186 Bedford Avenue

If you get frisky at the thought of whiskey, Spike Hill on Bedford is your jam. Speaking of jams, this joint is also a kick-ass 150-person music venue where you can catch local talent almost every night of the week. Order a whiskey flight (four pours of assorted whiskeys, ranging from the good stuff to the *really* good stuff) and let the brown take you to dancey town. When you need a break, fall into one of Spike Hill's high-walled, private, dark booths (the perfect place to play some footsie).

SPRITZENHAUS
#bar #BeerHall #jenga
33 Nassau Avenue

Located right on the Williamsburg/Greenpoint border, Spritzenhaus is a giant beer garden serving up brewskies and sausage, of both the meat and in-the-pants varieties. This place is huge—good news considering the massive amounts of good-looking boys and fräuleins bonding over beers and brats. Communal tables make mingling easy, and if you don't like the view inside, try sitting outside on a nice day, while taking in the sights of nearby McCarren Park.

SPUYTEN DUYVIL
#bar #RareBeers #backyard
359 Metropolitan Avenue

Big ol' beer dorks will bust their beer nuts over Brooklyn's OG beer bar, Spuyten Duyvil. Since they specialize in rare and obscure Belgian and international beers, you'll be hard-pressed to find a familiar brew. And with six taps, one cask, and a ton of bottles to choose from, your beer goggles will stay firmly attached all night. Need to soak up some of those super-rare suds? Order a meat and cheese platter and call it a meal. Their backyard is filled with trees and seats, and the inside has a couple of elevated windowsill school desks to enjoy your beer while you watch the rest of the crowd like a perched eagle.

SURF BAR
#bar #FakeBeach #FruityDrinks
139 N. 6th Street

Brooklyn's not exactly known for its thriving surf culture, but that doesn't mean you can't dip your toes in the sand while sipping on a fruity drink out of a coconut in this urban paradise. Filled with a bunch of kitschy, tiki, and surf shit, and serving up beers and strong tropical cocktails with paper umbrellas, Surf Bar is the perfect spot to spend a warm afternoon, lounging in the backyard, pretending like the sand between your toes is actually on a beach. After a few of the specialty mojitos, you'll swear you can hear the waves crashing (it's a toilet flushing), so drink up.

THE GUTTER
#bar #bowling
200 N. 14th Street

If you've ever felt like getting all *Big Lebowski* on some place, the Gutter is the perfect spot. This place is both a dive bar and an eight-lane bowling alley. The two areas are separated by a windowed wall so either you're showing off your strikes and spares with snazzy shoes on, or you're sitting at the bar, looking at all the dumbass drunk kids trying to stay out of the gutter. Tell Ronnie that he's way out of his element, down a few White Russians (stick with beers, they're cheap here), and don't forget to rerack your balls.

THE LEVEE
#bar #dive #CheesePuffs #jenga
212 Berry Street

A neighborhood shithole, the Levee is a good place to cap off the night when you're too wasted to care about cleanliness and your quality standards are generally low. Not the absolute grimiest place around, but they do allow dogs to sit in people chairs right up at the bar. PBR is the top seller here, and cheese puffs are the (free) bar snack of choice. The beer and shot specials are ridiculous ($4-$5). If you've retained some motor skills, there are various games you can play like Jonga, broke down darts, and shitty-felted pool. Really, come here to stuff your face with cheese puffs until somebody drags you home.

THE SHANTY
#bar #distillery #gin
79 Richardson Street

At some point in everyone's life, they begin to like gin. To check in on your palate's progress, hit up the Shanty, a bar attached to a distillery that's got gin- and rye-based drinks down cold. A small, classy but not up the assy type joint, the Shanty is great for day-drinking. This is how you do it up proper: Go to the distillery on either Saturday or Sunday at 3:00 p.m., learn about the process, and look at all the cool booze paraphernalia; stay for the live music at 4:00 p.m., then settle into the Shanty to continue drinking with the gin pros well into the night.

UNION POOL
#bar #LiveMusic #FirePit #TacoTruck
484 Union Avenue

If you show up to Union Pool with a bathing suit and cap ready to go for a dip, you may be disappointed. If you show up to Union Pool any night of the week expecting live music, cheap drinks, and epic adventures, you'll be thrilled. Located a stone's throw from the BQE on Union Avenue in Williamsburg, Union Pool is extra awesome in the spring and summer months when you can sit next to hottie strangers in the gargantuan backyard, sip from canned beers, and feast from the resident El Diablo Taco Truck. Hit it on Monday nights, when the backroom hosts Reverend Vince Anderson and his Love Choir, a show that'll take you to church, then to hell and back.

VERBOTEN
#club #electronica
54 N. 11th Street

This popular party has been moving bodies underground for years and recently established a solid location in Williamsburg. Verboten is all about techno/house and recruits only the best DJs to bring those heavy beats to your ears. The space is a massive ten thousand square feet that used to be a metal shop, and is decked out in all the right rough things to set the mood. The dance floor is raised and massive (and used to belong to Thomas Edison, no joke!), the sound system is truly incredible, and there's a cozier bar next door (with their own subdued sound) should you need to take a breather.

WYTHE HOTEL
#RooftopBar #views #TreatYourself
80 Wythe Avenue

As if we needed further proof that we can't afford to live in Williamsburg, along comes a fancy hotel with fancy people, willingly standing in line to drink expensive cocktails on a rooftop. Now, before you make that scrunchy face, we should note that the rooftop has a full panoramic view of Manhattan and an amazing terrace where you can sit, drink your fancy-ass drink, and take it all in. The vibe is upscale Brooklyn (especially on the weekends)—think wannabe-model types, strategically disheveled dudes and dudettes trying their best to make $300 jeans look like garbage, and a few normals just there for the view. Scrape up some change if you want dibs on the models; Manhattan drink prices apply.

SOUTH SIDE

COFFEE AND BAKERIES

BEANER BAR
#coffee #DiaDeLosMuertos #tamales
447 Graham Avenue

If *Dia de los Muertos* always passes you by way too quickly, you can hold on to that ghoulish feeling perpetually at Beaner Bar, a place designed with the Mexican dead in mind. On the outskirts of Williamsburg under the BQE, walking into this small shop is like taking a psychedelic trip to a colorful celebration, with heavily decorated walls plastered in ornate skeletal figurines, bright-colored paintings, and random photographs. The espresso machine and skilled barista sit smack in the middle of the joint, so starting up a little small talk is inevitable. This coffee shop also sells tamales, fresh, every day.

BLACK BRICK
#coffee #SchoolHouseFeel
300 Bedford Avenue

Black Brick looks like a rockabilly classroom. They serve up strongly brewed Stumptown, which you can enjoy in two areas: the open front atop tables made out of old rulers, or the dimly lit back where laptops rule. There is an exposed brick wall that runs throughout the joint to give it that old Brooklyn vibe, and the baristas, while short and to the point, are knowledgeable and friendly (but won't suck you into small-talk conversation). The place is rounded out with a cool ceiling that's made up of hammered-together crates.

EAT

BOZU
#sushi #TreatYourself #TokyoFeel
296 Grand Avenue

This joint is Japanese both in décor and cuisine—think fancy sushi with a twist. We're not talking some bogus tempura "I'm afraid to eat raw fish" kind of twist, but there's enough on the menu to find something for even the least fishy among us (the pork betty is a must). For you vegheads, the Ramo sushi roll kicks ass. From the front, the restaurant doesn't look like much, but once you're inside it feels like some back alleyway to Tokyo . . . and there may just be enough tourists in there to complete the illusion.

MARLOW & SONS
#TreatYourself #oysters #rustic
81 Broadway Avenue

A rustic place with damn good oysters. For $10 you get a half dozen oysters, and thirty seconds after they come to the table they'll be down your throat. Great for breakfast and dinner, their menus change frequently and only feature a few well-prepared items with nuanced flavors. For the morning, their egg-and-cheese biscuit (to which you can add bacon or sausage) is light, fluffy, and amazing. For dinner, the brick chicken is crisp on the outside, with succulent juices inside. It's a place where you'll want to get wine with your meal, but we warn you: If you're the type that can't just keep it to one glass, your bill will be astronomical.

MOTORINO
#pizza #wine #FamousFood
139 Broadway Avenue

As far as rock star pizza goes, this one is up there with Jagger, with other locations in the East Village, Manila, and Hong Kong. From sauce to crust and the carefully selected ingredients riding on top, the delicate balance of flavors and textures at Motorino never disappoint. You'd think all this fussed-over pizza would come from years of Italian family traditions, but you'd be wrong. The owner, Mathieu Palombino, is a Belgian guy obsessed with the pizza pie. From the simple Marinara ($10) to the spicy-sausage sprinkled Pugliese ($17), each pizza is made with the love of one hundred (Belgian) nonnas. The guy's even figured out the perfect pizza wine ($9 per glass) to go with your foreign, yet somehow perfectly authentic pizza-eating experience.

RYE
#brunch #TreatYourself #1920sTheme
247 S. 1st Street

This one's a splurge but well worth it. Travel back in time to when tin ceilings and suspenders were the norm, and suck down an old man's drink made with the restaurant's namesake. Brunch here is incredible, but Rye is best experienced at night when the lights go down and the antique mirrors behind the bar make you feel like you're on the set of *Boardwalk Empire*. If you decide on brunch, don't miss the Rye Benedict (made with pork belly, for chrissake), and if you're thinking cheapish dinner, we recommend the cauliflower gratin or meatloaf sandwich.

TRAIF
#TreatYourself #RebelRestaurant
#FamousFood
229 S. 4th Street

Traif (also spelled trayf, treyf, etc.) is a Yiddish word that refers to anything unkosher. The fact that this Williamsburg joint flaunts dirty, dirty pork and shellfish in a highly Orthodox Jewish hood gives this establishment some rebel juju. The chef's tasting menu is worth the splurge at $45—which is still pretty damn cheap by NYC standards. Tiny portions are what Traif does best. An outdoor garden can make you forget you're dining right by the mouth of the Williamsburg Bridge.

XIXA
#TreatYourself #dinner
#ReimaginedMexican
241 S. 4th Street

This will be the oddest Mexican food you've ever had, probably because it was conceived by two very non-Mexicans. Jason Marcus and Heather Heuser, the owners of the wildly popular next-door restaurant Traif, threw a double-down on Xixa (pronounced "shiksa"). Traif is both a restaurant and a love (and life) story told through food and wine. Jason (the Jew) and Heather (the shiksa) are avid travelers and pretty fucking imaginative people. They decided to open a parallel restaurant that would also tell a semifictitious food story that asks the eater to pretend that the chef was born in Mexico City. As such, Xixa serves some wild Mexican (-inspired) food. You'll find familiar spicy and sweet flavors, white cheeses, guac, and salsas, but also in the mix you'll get risottos, Italian chorizo, Brussels sprouts, foie gras, and edamame. This sounds like a clusterfuck of things, but trust us, it works. You'll spend a pretty penny in Mexican fairytale land, but this will be a very unique experience bolstered by their beverage program, which focuses on agave, hops, and grapes.

ZIZI LIMONA
#Mediterranean #BabaGhanoush
#SlowCookedMeat #SaucesForSale
129 Havemeyer Street

All that stuff you're used to eating from street carts is dressed up at Zizi Limona, a super-romantic restaurant that condenses the bold flavors of Middle Eastern and Mediterranean cuisines into small, filling portions. Dedicated to a cultural mix of Israeli, Moroccan, and Turkish, Zizi makes you feel warm and cozy with its slow-cooked meats, dimly lit interior, and inviting décor. Your usual Mediterranean suspects are done up to perfection here: the shawarma is so well spiced, the hummus is perfectly creamy, the falafel is crispy, and the lamb kofta is juicy and wonderful. There's also this pomegranate sauce that you'll want to buy by the bucketful (and luckily they have jars of it for sale at their in-store mini-market).

5 BEST BRUNCHES

The big spot in the 'burg for brunch used to be Egg. But the place has moved, the line is still long, and the goods aren't as great. Have a better brunch experience at these five.

FIVE LEAVES

The mason jar mecca of Brooklyn, Five Leaves (18 Bedford Avenue) is all about old-timey flair. While they've got the whole day covered (with an "in-between" menu should you wake up at 3:00 p.m. and not know what to call that meal), their weekend brunch is what puts them on the map in this picky-eater part of town. Their ricotta pancakes are huge, fluffy, and with the ricotta peeking through in every bite. The Moroccan scramble, with spicy merguez sausage, is perfect if you need to be hit in the face with flavor to wake up in the morning. They've got nicely flavored cocktails, the servers are all attentive (with great tattoos), and the atmosphere is that of fresh, airy light seeping in through their many windows and the sound of lightly clinking cups.

CAFE MOGADOR

When was the last time you sat down to eat Moroccan eggs Benedict in a tranquil indoor patio surrounded by lush foliage and models? Welcome to Cafe Mogador (133 Wythe Avenue)—home of reasonable, delicious, fresh Moroccan and Mediterranean food and the hottest people on the planet eating it. For over thirty years, Cafe Mogador has been an East Village staple, drawing huge crowds to a restaurant the size of a little person's shoebox. In 2012, the same owners opened Cafe Mogador Brooklyn—the better-looking younger sister, with the same menu and sense of style as her older sibling.

LE BARRICOU

Le Barricou (533 Grand Street) is an off-the-beaten-path French restaurant, serving country-style French food so good you'll be going *oui oui* all the way home (try the lamb ragout, little piggie). Serving lunch, dinner, and weekend brunch (the goddamn fluffiest pancakes you've ever seen) in a casual but slightly upscale environment, Le Barricou is the kind of place you put on real pants for. Once seated, we suggest you go straight for the jugular and order a shrimp Bloody Mary. With their wooden shelves and country furniture, the sun-waterfall that comes through the skylight, and elegant mirrors, this place feels fancy without being dickish.

PIES-N-THIGHS

Sorry, Southerners Brooklyn's got you beat when it comes to chicken. We even know one Virginia boy who decided to stay in NYC once he had dined at Pies-n-Thighs (166 S. 4th Street). This hole-in-the-wall (complete with red-and-white-checked tablecloths, plastic baskets of biscuits, and diner-style glasses of Coca-Cola) seriously serves up the best damn fried chicken that'll ever grease your fingers. While the simple chicken biscuit makes us salivate at mere thought, the other half of the joint's namesake (the pies!) are well worth the trip alone. Don't skimp on the sides either; the spicy black-eyed-pea salad will forever change the way you think about beans. This is a brunch you'll need to have with a side of nap.

BATTERY HARRIS

We're confident you can get your $25 worth of bottomless brunch at this spot. You get one entrée (the choices for which are classic brunch items but with a Caribbean jerk twist), coffee, and as many mimosas or Bloody Marys as you can get down in the two-hour time frame. This airy Rockaway Beach-inspired oasis under the BQE was a much needed addition to the hood when it opened in 2013. One of the most unique layouts in NYC, Battery Harris (64 Frost Street) features an indoor-outdoor bar serving up rare cocktails (don't miss the Dark and Stormy "Frozie," which isn't included in the brunch special) and the best Caribbean jerk this side of Harlem. There's a wood-burning stove out back, so in the winter you can get your nicotine fix without freezing. In addition to brunch, the bar hosts events—ranging from crazy cheap drink specials to brass-band concerts to live DJ sets—almost every night of the week.

HONORABLE MENTION

HOUSE OF SMALL WONDER

The House of Small Wonder (77 N. 6th Street) feels like you're hanging out at your fashionable friend's house, and the real wonder here is the tree growing right through the middle. There are a lot of plants and open spaces to soothe your partied-too-hard soul, and the brunch here is light, fresh, and will gently nudge you toward recovery. Their focus is on quality flavors; as such the menu is short and easy to navigate. A Euro-Japanese fusion, you'll find croissants, great cheese, sashimi, and udon, all of which are fantastic. Brunch is served all day, every day, making the House of Small Wonder the perfect weekday hangover cure.

SEE AND DO

MAGIC COBRA TATTOO SOCIETY
#StyleVariety #BestFlash
#FridayThirteenthDeal
775 Driggs Avenue

An excellent shop to hit if you're just starting to conceptualize your idea, Cobra is home to a diverse collection of artists who will hook you up with something traditional and timeless (you must book with legend Joe Truck), some new-school concoction, or a mix of styles (Woodz's work is impressive in that category). Whether you're coming in for a sleeve or a butterfly (please don't), the Cobra is always a good, lively experience. Many shops offer a cheap tat every Friday the thirteenth ($20 here), but the Cobra has the best flash sheet we've seen, so you don't have to get stuck with something fugly for being frugal. They run specials all the time and have a great sense of humor.

THE MUSE BROOKLYN
#acrobats #CrazyCircusShit #classes
32D S. 1st Street

A variety-show venue, the Muse was built by a community of artists and puts on a lot of fun circus shows, sometimes with acrobats, sometimes with burlesque dancers. Keeping it super funky, this place is a combo of Cirque du Soleil skills and weirder-than-weird imaginations. Come here to see a mind-blowing show (the Halloween ones are amazing) or hone your own carney craft (juggling classes are $18 each).

🏪 SHOP

BROOKLYN INDUSTRIES OUTLET
#clothes #deals #BKPrintedShirts
184 Broadway Avenue

Those overworn Brooklyn logo shirts can usually be traced back to Brooklyn Industries, and most poor bastards sporting said shirts paid way too much for their piece of the BK. We'd never let you pay full price for this shit. The BK Industries Outlet store is great because their played-out shirts are an affordable $10-$12, the J.Crew-chic threads are from their recent lines, and you can afford to buy a good-quality jacket to keep you warm when the New York winter sneaks up on you.

LA DI DA DEE
#trendy #affordable
184 Broadway Avenue

A good place to go to keep up with this fashionable hood, La Di Da Dee sells new on-trend threads for a good price. It's a small shop but the inventory always keeps up with the time. Here, you'll find sexy weekend dresses, nice brunch-weather skirts, and sweaters for when it gets chilly. Their accessories, heavy on geometric and bold gold pieces, will help you stand out in the blinged-out crowd. Come here with at least $50 to spend.

PARTYING

BABY'S ALL RIGHT
#DinnerAndShow
146 Broadway Avenue

The "dinner and show" idea, updated to fit our supercool needs, Baby's All Right has a little restaurant up front and a really nicely lit performance area in the back. The eats here are perfect for fueling for the show to come. From doorman to bartenders, the staff is super nice and doesn't push you around like cattle. Their lineup tends to consist of high-energy performers, their bigger shows sell out quick, and the sound is excellent. If you get a chance to look down, the floor between the two rooms has the maze from *The Shining* painted on it, because they're cool like that.

EAST RIVER BAR
#bar #bikers #patio #pool
#BigBuckHunter
97 S. 6th Street

Someone once told us that they saw Beyoncé here, maybe circa 2009. If that doesn't make you drop everything and run to East River Bar, perhaps you can be enticed with supercheap beers, a nice big patio (where you can BYOBBQ) that sits right under the Manhattan Bridge, drunk dudes hovering over the Big Buck Hunter, and mid-'90s hot jams blasting on most nights. Since the place is a little out of the way, it never gets too crowded and attracts a lot of (nice, really drunk) regulars. The big focal point here is their pool table, on an elevated area with proper elbow room. A whatever's clever type bar, East River is most definitely a dive.

OTB
#bar #HorseRaceTheme
#oysters #cocktails
141 Broadway Avenue

The kind of place you go when you've just cleaned under your fingernails, any bar with a legit chandelier is classy by our standards (and OTB's got a couple). With its booths, club chairs, whimsical horse images, and a few pieces of racing memorabilia, the place is decorated to evoke the Off Track Betting (OTB) culture of the '30s. As nice as it is inside, they're not out to rip you off. Come here on a Monday for $1 oysters and have a few of their super balanced cocktails (all only $10). Inside a green file folder bearing the words "Alcohol Incident Log" you will find the menu includes a list of "classic" cocktails your granddad drank (like the again popular old-fashioned) and a list of "modern" quirky mixes like the mezcal-heavy "Staycation." All bets point to yes.

POST OFFICE
#bar #PostalTheme
#GrilledCheese #cocktails
188 Havemeyer Street

Subtly sticking to the name's theme, this bar's menu is a postal envelope, the wallpaper behind the bar is all about American eagles, and (just because we have to get the pun out of the way) the Post Office really delivers when it comes to a wide selection of nice whiskeys, well-crafted cocktails, and new takes on American bar food. We had the Jersey Fire Drill and that shit was spicy, with its hellfire habanero bitters. We chased it with a grilled cheese...with bacon.

Always get it with bacon. Once you dip that perfectly toasty, melty delicious son-of-a-bitch into the little side of tomato soup that comes with it, you'll forget that you came here to get drunk.

THE TRASH BAR
#bar #dive #LiveMusic
256 Grand Street

Unlike the facial hair throughout most of Williamsburg, Trash Bar's name is far from ironic—this place is really a lovable shithole. The drinks are cheap, they serve greasy drunk food, and the décor is all trucker-stop chic (you might want to rethink sitting there). This dump is also a trashy music venue, and if you pay to see a band from seven to eight on Friday and Saturday night, or eight to nine Sunday through Thursday, this fine establishment rewards you with an open bar. When it comes to awesome dives, this trash is a treasure.

THE WOODS
#bar #DanceParty #backyard
48 S. 4th Street

You know how you see all those hot hipster girls on the street, torn up from the night before, and wonder where the hell they're getting down so hard? It's the Woods (and probably some skeezy apartment parties bookending the night). The place is split into three areas for eaters, dancers, and smokers. The music is a catchall mix to get everyone tapping their feet. It's the type of place where you go to dance for hours, even if it means occasionally getting reamed into the wall. The outdoor patio is like a club of its own, heated and with a taco truck that slings food you can enjoy during dance breaks. We're not sure if The Woods is trying to get people laid, but we've never left empty-handed.

DAY TRIPS

With its amazing food, artisan markets, street art, and wild parties, it's easy to get trapped in the Brooklyn bubble. You don't have to go far (or leave the borough) to feel like you're getting away. From nearby food-fantasy Queens to Atlantic City, there are many interesting things to do outside of the main drag. The beach, snow-covered slopes, and the nation's capitol are only a bus ride away. There's also this little thing called Manhattan right across the bridge. Here are a few ideas to get you out of dodge for a while.

GOVERNOR'S ISLAND

If it's summertime and the air is fine, hop on the weekend ferry ($2) at Pier 6 (Brooklyn Bridge Park) or take the R train to Whitehall Street and step off into an odd colonial world, floating in between skyscraper-ridden Manhattan and funky-fresh Brooklyn. Open only Fridays, Saturdays, and Sundays, Governor's has a fake beach (with real sand), bike rentals (free for an hour on Fridays), hammocks in the picnic area (choice real estate, so get yours early), and rocking chairs if you dig deep.

MANHATTAN ("THE CITY")

Chances are, even if you're all about Brooklyn, you'll still hit the city at some point (it'd be stupid not to). The best way to get there is across the Brooklyn Bridge, where not only will your feet hit iconic pavement, but your eyes will also be treated to a postcard view of lower Manhattan. At ground level, you'll find yourself amid the architectural charm of government buildings and City Hall Park, and within a short walk from Tribeca. Swing up Broadway and get lost in Chinatown, where vendors hawk crazy shit on every square inch of sidewalk. Going east will throw you in the mix with the models, artists, and weirdos of the East Village. In this pick-your-own-adventure sort of city, you'll want to do some touristy stuff, even if it means just lounging at Union Square or any of the iconic parks (Washington Square, Central, Madison Square, the High Line, and other patches of green New Yorkers call parks). If your legs give out, remember that while it's packed full of action, the island is small, and there will always be a subway nearby to take you back to Brooklyn (where you belong!).

FIRE ISLAND

A big gay beach destination, Fire Island is a place many New Yorkers head every summer for some rest, relaxation, and a few roaming deer. This is the kind of beach where the less you wear, the better.

BEACH BUSES

For a Jacob Riis beach getaway, you can hop on the A train and ride that lonely sucker down to beach town, or you can hook up with the party (school) bus; two actually. The NYC Beach Bus runs to the Rockaway boardwalk and Riis Beach several times a day on both Saturday and Sunday, has two pickup locations (Park Slope and Williamsburg), and will only cost you $12 round trip. Their competitor, the more established Rockabus, will get you there for $15 and departs from Grand Army Plaza and Williamsburg. The extra $3 will get you an upgraded stereo system with local DJs showcasing their fresh mix tapes.

OTP Tip: If you're the surfing type, the Rockaways offer up some good Atlantic waves, and Boarders Surf Shop (192 Beach 92nd Street) will hook you up with everything you need to get started. Hit the Rockaway Beach Surf Club (302 87th Street) afterward to drink with local surfers.

SNOW BUS

From December to March, the NYC Snow Bus makes getting out of the city for a quick snowboarding trip really easy. All you do is buy your ticket ($35 for bus, $67 for bus and lift pass, $97 for the whole shebang plus equipment rentals), hop on the bus at 8:00 a.m. (from Barclays Center or under the BQE in Williamsburg), and sit back while the bus takes you to Mountain Creek in New Jersey. Upon return, you can cap off the day at one of the bus company's partner beer-slingers for a little discounted booze.

SPA CASTLE

For $40 ($50 on the weekends), you can basically pamper yourself into a gelatinous state. Getting there is super easy: Just hop on the 7 train and ride it to the last stop, where a shuttle bus awaits to take you to paradise. In addition to jets, waterfalls, and submerged loungers, they also offer massages, smoothies, food, and facials for reasonable prices.

BOSTON

Going to Beantown is as easy as hopping on a bus. You have three choices here: the rickety wild ride on the Chinatown bus that transports mostly humans but sometimes chickens, and the Megabus or BoltBus, which are comparatively more comfortable options that often run great discount deals to Boston, which means you can get a round-trip ticket for under $10 if you're lucky.

PHILLY

The cheesesteaks in NYC not authentic enough? Ship out to Philly for the real deal. If you hop on the Chinatown bus, you can get there for $12 round trip. For something a little cushier (and not necessarily more expensive), book a ticket at off-peak hours with Megabus (or BoltBus) to get there for under $5.

ATLANTIC CITY

Got cash to burn? Want to do it in the riskiest way possible? Atlantic City is nearby to turn your money into a distant memory. The model city for the über-capitalist board game Monopoly, Atlantic City isn't Vegas, but on the East Coast, it's the next best thing. For $40 round trip (a little less on weekdays), Academy Bus lines will take you from Port Authority to the heart of the oldest boardwalk in the United States in about two hours.

QUEENS

Popularized by the "Outer Boroughs" episode of Bourdain's No Reservations, Queens is filled with the kind of food that draws adventurous eaters from all over the world. There are thousands of vendors hawking everything under the sun. Jeffrey Tastes (the "Queens Qustodian") runs his own food tour that'll help you focus when your eyes go wandering and your stomach is growling. He knows all the vendors personally. Google him.

AUTHOR BIOS

ANNA STAROSTINETSKAYA

Anna is the editor-in-chief of Off Track Planet and has been happily in charge of content production from day one. Born in the former USSR, her passion for travel began early in life when her family left the Union, first stopping in Austria and Italy before settling in Los Angeles in 1990. After a long stint in LA, Anna moved to Brooklyn in 2009 and cofounded Off Track Planet. A homeless man once told her that it takes five years to become a true Brooklynite. While she hit that anniversary in 2014, Anna still feels like every day in Brooklyn is new and unique. She wrote this guide to help people discover the magic of this crazy city for themselves.

FREDDIE PIKOVSKY

Freddie is the CEO of Off Track Planet and has his hands in every aspect of the company. Freddie was born in Brooklyn, grew up in Los Angeles, but returned to Brooklyn in 2009 where he started *Off Track Planet* from a hostel dorm room after an inspiring backpacking trip across Europe. Freddie is responsible for the production and direction for this guidebook. His most recent adventure was completing a solo trip on his vintage motorcycle across the U.S.A, stopping off at every bookstore along the way to sign and snap photos of OTP's first book entitled *Off Track Planet's Travel Guide for the Young, Sexy, and Broke.*

CONTRIBUTORS

CHRISTOPHER PLATIS

Chris is originally from Greece, where he recently opened a boutique hotel. One of OTP's first writers and editors, Chris contributed his vast knowledge and childhood memories of Bay Ridge to this book. He is a brilliant man with excellent hair and posture.

LISETTE CHERESSON

Lisette was OTP's first senior editor and is never in one place for too long. She's explored thirty countries and recently returned to New York after a fifteen-month backpacking trip. For this book, Lisette contributed her expertise on eateries and watering holes in Williamsburg and Bushwick. Her documentary production company, Flyover Pictures, has produced fourteen short pieces around the world and is currently in production on a full-length film.

SARA M. WHITE

Sara is a seasoned OTP writer, and while she lived in Brooklyn for a while, she has hopped coasts to pursue her career in screenwriting at UCLA. Before she left, Sara threw some gems our way, contributing reviews of her favorite neighborhood bars and restaurants in Williamsburg. Hollywood better watch out! This girl is going to be big time.

PHOTO CREDITS

p. 6: L. Latumahina; p. 11 (blackout riots, right): Dick DeMarsico; p. 11 (Biggie Smalls, center): Bad Boy Records; p. 11 (Hurricane Sandy, right): Master Sgt. Mark C. Olsen; p. 13: Jafar; pp. 14, 15, 27 (Bay Ridge Ave) 29, 35, 37, 39, 40, 42, 43, 46–49, 50, 51, 60, 61 (lox and bagel), 63, 65, 66, 67, 69, 70 (Brooklyn Kolache Co.), 71, 72 (Do or Dine), 74 (Speedy Romeo), 76 (Ol' Dirty Bastard Mural), 77, 85, 86, 88, 89, 91, 96, 97 (Juliana's), 99, 100, 101, 102, 103, 105 (market exterior), 107, 113, 115 (Fort Greene tower), 116, 120, 121, 130, 137, 140, 142, 158, 181, 183, 185, 187, 188, 191, 197 (Mast Brothers Chocolate, bottom right), 210: Freddie Pikovsky; p. 17: Michael Mandiberg; p. 19: Timothy Vollmer; p. 20 (top): Shawn Perez; p. 20 (bottom): Adam Jones; p. 21 (band, upper left): Bill Ebbesen; p. 21 (guy with guitar, bottom left): Kevin N. Murphy; p. 21 (pork buns, upper right): Shellack; p. 21 (challah, lower right): Aviv Hod; p. 22: Christian Razukas; p. 23 (guy sitting, left): Joel Bedford; p. 23 (girls walking, right): Dilia Oviedo; p. 25: Kris Arnold; p. 27 (pizza shop): Rebecca Wilson; p. 27 (Chevy Impala): Michael Dolan; p. 28 (Robicelli's): Chun Yip So; p. 28 (The Coffee Lab): Salim Virji; p. 30 (tacos, left): Arnold Gatilao; p. 30 (tacos, right): Michael Saechang; p. 31: Dave Herholz; p. 32: Krista; p. 33: Adam Joyce Andes; pp. 34, 72 (Crown Fried Chicken), 74 (Scratch Bread), 75, 76 (Met food market), 117, 128, 160, 161: Tanair Gaines; p. 38: mike aka mlcastle; p. 45: Kowarski; p. 52: IntangibleArts; p. 53: (Silent Barn, top): Ethan M. Long; p. 53 (Silent Barn, bottom): Georgia aka georgia.kral; p. 55: MephistoPuck; p. 57: Spyder Monkey; p. 58: Jessica Spengler; p. 59: New Amsterdam Market; p. 61 (Lucali): Eric Mueller; p. 61 (Peter Shelsky): Meng He; p. 62: andikas881; p. 64 : Bonniekate; p. 70 (Dough): John "star5112"; p. 78: Christina Goedecke; p. 79: Florence Y; p. 81: Steven Pisano; p. 83: Daniel Fleming; p. 84: Mr. TinDC; p. 87: Hypnotica Studios Infinite; p. 93: Quinn Dombrowski; p. 95: Ludovic Bertron; p. 97 (Grimaldi's): William J. Sisti; p. 105 (foliage): Jasoninbklyn; p. 106: Jim McGaw; p. 108: e.t; p. 109 (beef patty, top): Jason Lam; p. 109 (jerk chicken, bottom left), Naotake Murayama; p. 109 (jerk chicken, bottom right) and p. 165 Stu Spivack; p. 111 (Di Fara, top): Joey aka joooey; p. 111 (Di Fara exterior): apasciuto; p. 112: Olaf Tausch; p. 115 (Fort Greene Park crowd): Cesar Perdomo; p. 115 (buildings): Francisco Daum; p. 118: Jeffrey Barry; p. 119: David Shankbone; p. 123 (Flea, top): dumbonyc; p. 123 (Flea, bottom left): Eli Duke; p. 123 (suitcases): Kristen Taylor; p. 123 (crowd, bottom right): Evanscott7; p. 125: Steven Pisano; p. 126: Jacques Renier; p. 127 (tacos): Evan P. Cordes; p. 127 (croissant): Sundar1; p. 131: Ben Sisto; p. 132 (Littlefield): Heather M. Kendrick; p. 132 (Mission Dolores Bar): Mission Dolores Bar; p. 133: Jon Wilde; p. 135 (woman with bicycle, top left): Matt Jiggins; p. 135 (Manhattan Ave, top right): The All-Nite Images; p. 135 (picnic, bottom left): Keren Richter; p. 135 (bar, bottom right): gt8073a; p. 138: Jason Eppink; p. 139: THOR; p. 141: Janne Hellsten; p. 143: Samat K Jain; p. 145: karlnorling; p. 148: Julie Corsi; p. 150: Jun Seita; pp. 151, 153, 199 (Mini-Mall), 200, 203: Chris Platis; p. 153: Talde; p. 155 (Prospect Park, top): MamboZ; p. 155 (boathouse, bottom): Vlad Iorsh; p. 156: Chris Phutully; p. 157: Jeffrey O. Gustafson; p. 163 (Grand Army Plaza, left): Rich Mitchell; p. 163 (museum, right): Kim aka TheGirlsNY, p. 167: Steve Soblick; p. 169: Scott Dexter; p. 170: Rich Mitchell; p. 171: Le Living and Co.; p. 172: Cocktail Marler; p. 173: The Way Station; p. 175: Sunghwan Yoon; p. 176: Kristen Taylor; p. 178: Michael Minn; p. 179: Brewbooks; p. 180 (bartender, left): Max Kelly; p. 180 (wide shot, top): Eatery Row; p. 180 (cocktail, bottom): Geoff Peters; p. 190: Jerk Alert Productions; p. 194: Linaduliban; p. 195 (zucchini salad cone, right): Erin aka Erin & Camera; p. 195 (oyster party, top left): Vincent Lim Show Chen; p. 195 (Mexican sandwich, bottom left): bolbolaan; p. 196: Kent Westlund; p. 197 (Brooklyn Night Bazaar, top right and left): Brooklyn Night Bazaar; p. 197 (Brooklyn Brewery, bottom left): Bernt Rostad; p. 199 (The Meat Hook): Gary Stevens; p. 205: Vladimir; p. 206: Mark Mahaney; p. 207: Beaner Bar; p. 208: Motorino; p. 211: Le Barricou; p. 212: JIP; p. 213: Corey O'Day; p. 215: Ellen Ordóñez

INDEX